THE REAL READE

Slightly Foxed

'A Crowning Achievement'

NO.57   SPRING 2018

Editors Gail Pirkis & Hazel Wood
Marketing and publicity Stephanie Allen & Jennie Harrison Bunning
Bookshops Anna Kirk
Subscriptions Hattie Summers, Olivia Wilson & Katy Thomas

Cover illustration Luke Martineau, *Westminster, Afternoon Light* (detail)
Luke Martineau was educated at Eton and Oxford and then studied briefly at the Heatherley
School of Fine Art in London before beginning to paint professionally. His versatile output
encompasses portraiture, landscape, still life and illustration. He discovered a passion for landscape painting at an early age, and *plein air* painting, whether on his travels or in London, is
still an important part of his work. His paintings are held in many public and private collections including the Royal Collection. Luke is also President of the Chelsea Arts Society. For
more of his work visit www.panterandhall.com.

Design by Octavius Murray
Layout by Andrew Evans
Colophon, tailpiece and back cover fox by David Eccles

Contents

Contents

John Watson

For the digital edition of *Slightly Foxed* and an up-to-date list of partners
and membership benefits, please visit the members' page on our website:
www.foxedquarterly.com/members or contact Olivia:
olivia@foxedquarterly.com · +44 (0) 20 7033 0258

The Slightly Foxed office can obtain all books reviewed in this issue,
whether new or second-hand. Please contact Anna:
anna@foxedquarterly.com · +44 (0) 20 7033 0258

From the Editors

So, spring again, and it seems a good moment to report on what might be called the greening of *Slightly Foxed*. We've always been keen to be green and during the past year we've worked hard at it, replacing our plastic-lined padded envelopes with more eco-friendly cardboard packaging and looking into switching our office paper to a more environmentally friendly brand called Cool Earth.

In his wickedly funny book *A Boy at the Hogarth Press* (now available, by the way, as a Plain Foxed Edition), Richard Kennedy reveals that Leonard Woolf kept a keen eye on the consumption of everything in the Hogarth Press office, including the loo paper. We don't go quite that far, but needless to say, we make sure what we buy is recycled. In fact we now recycle pretty well everything that's possible, and our recycling firm sends encouraging reports on how many trees we've saved (21 last year). Plastic water bottles are banned in the office and, at a more personal level, Alarys – who has now moved on from *SF* to greater things – gathers our office shredding as winter bedding for her tortoise, while Olivia saves postage stamps to send to her grandma who collects them for charity.

It's a drop in the ocean, but it all adds up, and with the world so out of kilter it feels good to be doing something constructive. And, at the risk of being boring, may we mention yet again another small but important thing, which is to try to support small businesses like independent bookshops who employ local people and pay their rates and taxes, rather than greedy giants like Amazon. But we'd better not get started . . .

Last year we thought we'd arrived at a point where there were no more Carey novels left to reissue. So it was very exciting to learn that lying among Ronald Welch's papers, forgotten for 30 years, was the manuscript of a previously unseen short novel, which we're now able to publish for the first time.

The Road to Waterloo is every bit as colourful and realistic as the other Carey novels and though not officially part of the series, it fills a significant gap in the family story. The setting is June 1815, Napoleon has recently escaped from Elba and its young hero James Carey, a Cornet in the 30th Light Dragoons and part of Wellington's great allied army, is patrolling the Franco-Belgian border, on the lookout for the arrival of Napoleon's troops. James is only 17 and this is his first experience of active service. As always skilfully mixing fact and fiction, Welch gives us a vivid and fascinating picture of the days leading up to the final great battle and of a young soldier's coming of age. *The Road to Waterloo* is available to order now, in the same handsome Cubs format and with specially commissioned illustrations by Mark Robinson.

Both in his person and in his writing the adventurous traveller Eric Newby was an unusually elegant man, so perhaps it is not entirely surprising to learn that he began his career in fashion – as an inept post-war trainee at the family firm of Lane & Newby, 'Mantle Manufacturers and Wholesale Costumiers'. This is the story he tells in *Something Wholesale*, our latest Slightly Foxed Edition (see p.13). Newby is always at his funniest when at a disadvantage, and his account of his hapless attempts at salesmanship and of the gradual collapse of the tottering family firm is a treat.

And finally, many congratulations to the winner of our ninth crossword competition, Mrs K. J. Meakin, who receives a free annual subscription. For anyone who was stumped, the answers are on p.95.

GAIL PIRKIS & HAZEL WOOD

A Crowning Achievement

JANE RIDLEY

Like so many *Slightly Foxed* readers, I was hooked by Netflix's first series of *The Crown*. The lavish production, rumoured to have cost £100 million, the understated acting, the meticulous detail and the cut-glass accents – all gave each episode a sense of stunning authenticity. Claire Foy, in the role of the Queen, was immaculate and as compelling as anyone can be driving a Land Rover in twinset and pearls, and the series as a whole introduced us to a world of privilege and glamour at the very heart of the British establishment which is usually shrouded in secrecy. But how accurate was it really?

One of the best guides to unscrambling fact from fiction is Ben Pimlott's biography *The Queen* (1996). Though published twenty years ago, this is still the defining historical account of Elizabeth II's first seventy years. The Queen was a strange subject for Pimlott to pick. Back in the 1990s the monarchy was not a topic considered worthy of serious academic study, let alone by a left-leaning contemporary historian such as Pimlott. A Labour activist and Birkbeck Professor of Politics who lived in Islington, he was the author of well-received lives of Hugh Dalton and Harold Wilson. Writing about the monarchy might well have been career-ending.

Nor was the biography easy to research. The Queen is one of the most famous and most photographed women in the world, but she gives no interviews, her archive is closed, and she is surrounded by a ring of silence. Pimlott recorded some interviews with people close to

Ben Pimlott, *The Queen: Elizabeth II and the Monarchy* (1996)
Harper Press · Pb · 816pp · £14.99 · ISBN 9780007476626

Queen Elizabeth II, 1952, by Dorothy Wilding
© NPG

her, but in 1996 few insiders were willing to talk. One solution to the lack of hard evidence would have been to publish all the gossip and be damned, as Kitty Kelley had done with her book *The Royals*. Pimlott, however, would never have dreamed of writing such a book. Instead he wrote a historical biography: a book which, as Elizabeth Longford observed, was 'an outstanding biography for a historian to have written, and an equally outstanding history to be written by a biographer'.

I first came across Pimlott's biography last year, when I was looking for a decent book about the Queen. After a year of rough handling on tubes, trains and aeroplanes, my second-hand paperback copy is now broken-backed and its pages are marked and falling out.

From the beginning I was entranced. Pimlott's story doesn't start, as royal biographies usually do, with a chapter of potted genealogy. It opens with an account of the General Strike, describing the Home Secretary Sir William Joynson-Hicks rushing to the bedside of the Duchess of York at 2 a.m. to attend the birth of a possible heir to the throne at a crucial point in negotiations with the unions. Rather than dig around for details on breastfeeding or midwives, Pimlott places the birth of Princess Elizabeth firmly in its historical context.

Pimlott was concerned as much with the British public's obsession with royalty as he was with the monarch herself. The book is 'about the Queen in people's heads, as well as at Buckingham Palace', and the section on the Queen's childhood is a good example of this. The standard source of information on this period is *The Little Princesses*, the book written by the royal governess Marion Crawford (Crawfie) in 1950. It's a sympathetic account, though it caused a storm when it was published for violating the royal code of secrecy. Pimlott's reading of Crawfie is acute. He identifies two contradictory myths about the young Princess Elizabeth. On the one hand, she was seen as the essence of normality – as Lilibet with her horses and her dogs, living an 'ordinary' life with her family at No. 145 Piccadilly. But she was also regarded as an exceptional child, blessed with prophylactic powers to 'cure' the ailing George V, her 'Grandpa England'. Lilibet's relationship with her gruff, short-tempered grandfather, leading him on all fours by his beard, seemed to symbolize the transition from age to youth in the royal succession.

In terms of timescale one cannot really compare Pimlott's zero-to-seventy biography with the first series of *The Crown*, which spans a time frame of less than a decade – from Elizabeth's marriage in 1947 to the beginnings of the Suez crisis in 1956. But *The Crown* is punctuated by flashbacks to scenes from the Abdication of Edward VIII in 1936 and from Elizabeth's childhood, growing up in the shadow of the Abdication as Heiress Presumptive. The effect is to make the point which Pimlott clearly articulates – namely, that the Abdication 'broke the spell' of monarchy and made the personal life of the sovereign a constitutional issue. It was the task of George VI to restore faith in the monarch's dedication to duty, and this dutiful, cipher model of monarchy was the one that Elizabeth learned from her father and that she was determined to carry on.

When royals transgressed, they were fair game for the media. Hence the importance of Princess Margaret. *The Crown* dwells at length on Margaret's doomed romance with the divorced Peter Townsend. Today, it seems a storm in a royal teacup. But back then it mattered because, as Pimlott explains, it broke the unwritten rule that the royals mustn't allow personal gratification to take precedence over duty, thus tarnishing the institution of monarchy. Although the Duke of Windsor is given a greater role in *The Crown* than he actually played at the time, he is there to make the same point: warped, petulant and frustrated, he is a cautionary tale about the danger of giving up duty for love. Princess Margaret's threatened marriage was the first problem over which the Queen was required to exercise her independent judgement, and in the series she is careful not to take sides and manages to remain outside the argument. Here too *The Crown* is accurate.

A central theme of Pimlott's book is the changing relationship between the monarchy and the media. Influenced perhaps by his wife, the media historian Jean Seaton, Pimlott wrote perceptively about the shifting balance of power between the monarchy and the BBC. In the early 1950s, the BBC grovelled before the monarchy and obeyed Palace instructions not to photograph the Queen. By the 1960s, as the monarchy lost its glamour and began to look dull and tweedy, the royals needed the BBC more than it needed them. Prince Philip invited the cameras in to follow the family for a year, and the 1969 film *Royal Family* showed the royals as ordinary people. In the most famous scene the Queen and her family are filmed cooking a barbecue by a loch. The film received ecstatic notices. Too late did the Palace realize that they had let the genie out of the bottle. As Pimlott put it, 'If royal "privacy" was no longer sacrosanct, why should its exposure be strictly on royalty's own terms?'

The Coronation, as Pimlott observes, was a transforming moment in the creation of a media monarchy. Both Elizabeth and Prince Philip, who was a modernizer, opposed the idea of admitting the

BBC cameras at first, but then Elizabeth changed her mind. The ceremony was watched by 27 million viewers, and it created an expectation of BBC coverage of all royal events.

The Coronation is the sort of subject where film can perhaps convey more than the written word. Episode 5 of *The Crown* begins with a flashback from Elizabeth's childhood, in this instance invented, when her father George VI, rehearsing his role, asks his 10-year-old daughter to play the part of the Archbishop at his Coronation and pretend to anoint him with holy oil. The anointing is the motif encapsulating the religion and mystery of monarchy. The television cameras were banned from that part of the service in which the Queen dons a plain white dress, the Garter knights put a canopy over her head and the Archbishop anoints her. The exclusion of the cameras is made plain by showing archive footage – with a commentary by the Duke of Windsor, watching it in Paris. But the irony, and cleverness, of the episode is that we, the viewers, are shown the anointing and taken right to the heart of the secret mystery of monarchy.

Given the intimacy of scenes such as this, it is startling to read in Pimlott that at the beginning of Elizabeth's reign the Lord Chamberlain's Office forbade representation on stage or screen of any British sovereign from Queen Victoria onwards. Not until 1968 were the rules scrapped. Making a film about a living monarch would have been unimaginable before that date.

When it comes to politics, as opposed to ceremony, Pimlott's historical heft gives him an authority which *The Crown* cannot match. On the Queen's relations with her prime ministers he is definitive. The resignation of Macmillan in 1963 was a turning-point. The Queen, who was pregnant with Prince Edward, visited the sick Macmillan in his hospital bed in what Pimlott describes as 'the most remarkable audience in modern monarchical history'. She allowed herself to be duped by Macmillan into agreeing to his choice of successor – thus bringing to an end forever the monarch's discretionary power over the mid-term appointment of a prime minister.

The jury is still out on the Queen's relations with Margaret Thatcher. On the basis of his interviews with politicians, Pimlott makes a convincing case that the two women loathed each other. The Thatcherites 'identified the Court with the old-style *noblesse oblige* paternalism and social deference, which it was their mission to sweep away'. The Queen on the other hand found Thatcher's excessively deep curtseys coupled with her increasingly grand manner hard to bear. She got on far better with Harold Wilson.

Pimlott takes the story up to 1996. When the paperback edition was published the following year, he observed: 'Already the atmosphere has changed from that of the flat, anti-deference, politically-expedient mid-1990s, and perceptions of the Monarchy are shifting as well.' Rather than add a new chapter, he preferred to leave the book as it was – an interpretation written at a particular moment in the reign. Ironically perhaps, it was his book on the Queen rather than his lives of Labour politicians that made him a public intellectual and constitutional authority.

Pimlott died of leukaemia aged 58 in 2004. Is his book obsolete? Since the 1990s, more palace insiders have been prepared to talk frankly, and the wealth of interview material that makes Sally Bedell Smith's 2012 biography of *Elizabeth the Queen* so valuable was not available to Pimlott. The decades since Diana's death have seen a palace revolution, and the emergence of a more informal, human style of monarchy. The code of secrecy has begun to fade, and the Queen herself has learned to reveal more emotion than hitherto. But as a historical interpretation, showing the centrality of the monarchy as a benign and civilizing force in British life, Pimlott's book cannot be bettered.

JANE RIDLEY is writing a biography of the Queen's grandparents, King George V and Queen Mary.

Misadventures in the Rag Trade

ARIANE BANKES

It remains one of the more surprising facts of life that the intrepid
traveller Eric Newby, who by the time I knew him had the weather-
beaten cragginess of a man only happy when halfway up the Hindu
Kush, should have carved out an earlier career astride the lower slopes
of haute couture. Everyone has to start somewhere, however, and he
put his first reluctant footprint on the fashion world as hapless gofer
in the family firm of Lane & Newby, 'Mantle Manufacturers and
Wholesale Costumiers', from which he rose, more by luck than by
judgement, to the dizzy heights of Worth Paquin, later plateauing out
into the sunny uplands of John Lewis in the incongruous position of
buyer of Ladies' Fashion.

Those early trials on the nursery slopes are the subject of *Something
Wholesale* (1962), a book the enjoyment of which is strictly in inverse
proportion to the experience of its author, for Newby was always the
butt of his own best jokes, and never more so than when flounder-
ing in an element entirely uncongenial to him. There is a sense of
foreboding from the first page as we begin to guess his unhappy fate:
demobbed and demoralized in 1945 after an eventful war (some of it
chronicled in *Love and War in the Apennines*), he is thrust by his
exasperated parents into the hungry maw of the family firm, which
proves an experience every bit as exacting as the conflict he has just
thankfully escaped.

But the charm of this book lies in more than its droll evocation of
ineptitude and eccentricity. There is an elegiac quality about it, a hint
of nostalgia for a time when business could be conducted in a wholly
idiosyncratic manner, reliant on relationships that were honed over

decades of familiarity (and possibly contempt) but that were never-theless indulgent of the vagaries of all concerned. Those days were already numbered and Newby records them in a tone of affectionate derision, but there is no doubt whatsoever that life at the sharp end is a whole lot duller now.

Who could compete these days with Newby's first office encounter, as he stood uneasily in the panelled reception area of Lane & Newby's Great Marlborough Street premises, waiting for his duties to be enumerated? From a tiny booth under the resplendent carved stair-case emanated breathless confidences of the 'I just don't like the way he . . . No! The other one's worse than he is' variety, before a long, silk-clad leg slid sinuously round the door.

Half-mesmerized, as a snake charmer who has allowed one of his charges to gain control of the situation, I watched the leg in which muscles rippled sleek and powerful as a boa-constrictor's . . . I began to experience that morbid sensation known to psychologists as the Death Wish. For a moment I could think of nothing more delectable than being crushed to pulp by this and its attendant member.

This tantalizing encounter was swiftly countermanded by a bracing welcome from the imposing Miss Gatling, Company Secretary, 'baring her teeth with a sudden accession of bonhomie that was most alarming', and the stern advice to 'watch your step!' with the siren under the staircase. The scene was set.

There is more than a touch of the surreal in Newby's world. One of his early duties as junior member of the Mantle Department was to cut off lengths of material to supply the various orders, the first of which was for a wool georgette coat, model name 'Desire', to encompass a Mrs Bangle of Leeds. With the majestic dimensions of 'Hips 62″. Bust 58″. Waist 55″', it was plain that this was no ordinary woman. 'How did she get like that in wartime?' Newby asked in wonderment, only to be told, 'Bless you, Mr Eric, that's nothing. We have much worse than that. It's something to do with armaments.'

The vagaries of the customers were as nothing compared to the eccentricities of the staff, erratically presided over by Newby's father. *Something Wholesale* is in part a hymn to this man, the unlikely hero of the piece. Already an elderly and irascible patriarch by the time young Eric was drafted in, he epitomized the Edwardian era of which he was one of the last extant examples. He was a chancer, an adventurer, even if most of his travels were undertaken to drum up more orders for day dresses in Budapest or to press a new consignment of overcoats on the Dutch. The demands of his business were never allowed to interfere, however, with his one great passion: for rowing, or sculling, or messing around in boats on the River Thames.

He lorded it on the river as he lorded it over the denizens of Great Marlborough Street: peremptory, autocratic and determined at all costs to have a good time, he spent his life adroitly getting out of self-inflicted scrapes, which included nasty tiffs with swans, swarms of wasps and other river users. Some of his greatest scorn was reserved for those who turned up in 'the wrong sort of clobber', an actionable offence to a man always impeccably turned out in white flannel trousers, white buckskin shoes and magnificent cream blazer, whatever the weather. This Edwardian rectitude in the matter of dress he applied to his business too, and with the aid of his loyal and long-suffering wife he managed to keep Lane & Newby going through testing times, when the impact of Chanel's Little Black Dress and other thrilling Parisian innovations should by rights have knocked the whole business swiftly into receivership.

The owner of that silk-clad leg, on closer acquaintance, turned out to be Lola, a particularly seductive member of staff with no thought in her head beyond men, and in particular young men like Eric. Even his father acknowledged her charms – 'That's a finely developed girl you have in your department' – before advising 'A good long trot, then a rub-down and a cold bath' to ward off the lusts of the flesh. Such measures were woefully inadequate, but intervention from on high came just in the nick of time, in the form of an invitation back to Italy where the faithful Wanda was awaiting him. It was Wanda who had helped Eric escape from captivity during the war, at great risk to both herself and her family, and he had fallen in love with this spirited and beautiful young girl, who, as he pointed out, 'would have made short work of Lola'.

Eric still needed an income, however, and once safely married he was back again at Great Marlborough Street, where it was generally agreed he should make the transfer from the sultry charms of Lola's Stockroom to the far healthier ambience of the Showroom, where Miss Stallybrass reigned supreme. There his chief mentor was the inscrutable Mr Wilkins, 'impassive as a mandarin, almost bald and a complete mystery'.

It was in the company of Mr Wilkins that Eric thankfully escaped the premises. Twice a year visits were made to the buyers of department stores to flog the Spring and Autumn collections. These visits were referred to in reverential tones as 'The Journey', and were gruelling in the extreme. In addition to the physical demands of lugging vast numbers of garments from Edinburgh to Glasgow (or vice versa) and thence on daylight raids to the Borders, before trundling down through the great industrial towns of the North to Nottingham, there were the exacting emotional and intellectual demands of setting one buyer off against another, extracting the maximum tribute from both, yet somehow keeping them all happy. The stakes were high, the margins slim, the difference between success and failure a mere hair's breadth – and all hinged on the fiendish mix of flattery, duplicity and sheer guile perfected over the decades by Mr Wilkins.

No résumé could possibly do justice to the split-second timing of this high-wire act and its ghastly blend of horror and hilarity. Mr Wilkins's Scrooge-like stinginess put paid to even the few creature comforts that might have smoothed their passage through the nether-world of post-war third-rate Northern hotels, and his intransigence nearly drove Newby mad. He survived – just – and returned to

London a wiser and much chastened man, where even his normally implacable father was moved to offer him a few days off.

It was a tribute to Newby *père*'s determination and dexterity that Lane & Newby staggered on well into the 1950s, when its nemesis came in the form of the tax inspector, and profits, premises and Mr Newby's beloved supply of port were all swept away on a tidal wave of debt. By that stage, however, Eric had plans for an expedition to the Hindu Kush, and the rest is travel history. His Waugh-ish account of that adventure propelled him into a new career as a writer which he combined for many years with a day job as travel editor of the *Observer*. He was irrepressible to the very end of his long and active life: I was not at all surprised to hear that when he and Wanda eventually moved from their lovely but rather remote house in Dorset to a new home in West Sussex, Eric – well into his eighties by then – was busy digging out their new swimming-pool.

ARIANE BANKES much enjoyed being Eric Newby's editor in the dim mists of the past. She runs a small arts festival in the Peak District and combines writing, reviewing and editing the Charleston Trust's magazine *Canvas* with a spot of curating, in a most congenial blend. An extended version of her article on *Something Wholesale* first appeared in *SF* no. 15.

Eric Newby's *Something Wholesale* (256pp) is now available in a limited and numbered cloth-bound edition of 2,000 copies (subscriber price: UK & Eire £16, Overseas £18; non-subscriber price: UK & Eire £17.50, Overseas £19.50). All prices include post and packing. Copies may be ordered by post (53 Hoxton Square, London N1 6PB), by phone (020 7033 0258) or via our website www.foxedquarterly.com.

Dying for a Dream

ROMESH GUNESEKERA

Many writers have places, real or imagined, linked with their names – Joyce's Dublin, Hardy's Wessex, Faulkner's Yoknapatawpha – but I don't know of any who have a province named after them, other than José Rizal, the Filipino author of *Noli Me Tangere*. The province of Rizal was created in 1901 (two years after the country was ceded to America by Spain), to honour the best-known martyr of Philippine nationalism. It stretches from the Laguna de Bay, the largest lake in the country, to the edge of Manila, the city my father moved to in the 1960s.

I followed as a migrant teenager from Ceylon, beginning to dream of writing but uninterested in history or national heroes. So my first encounter with Rizal's name was not on a page but in a car, driving through Rizal province to the Antipolo hills which look down on the city that had become my home.

In today's world, Manila may not seem so surreal, but in 1960s Asia the mix of a Spanish colonial heritage and American materialism was startling. The city had a distinctly Hispanic air to it, especially in the houses of the better-off, combined with more than a hint of the Wild West. American English was spoken in the malls, Spanish in the drawing-rooms. There was still a serious debate about what should be the national language, Spanish having been eclipsed by English and Tagalog. Society ladies in embroidered finery sipped coffee from elegant china, and not so far away American GIs on R&R from the war

José Rizal, *Noli Me Tangere* (1887) · Trans. Harold Augenbraum
Penguin · Pb · 464pp · £12.99 · ISBN 9780143039693

in Vietnam roamed the streets looking for hostess clubs and massage parlours. There was no other place quite like it, real or imagined.

A hundred years earlier, when the Philippines were still ruled by Spain, José Rizal was startled by Manila for very different reasons. He came to the city from his home town of Calamba to study at Ateneo, a prestigious Jesuit school and university. His family was well-to-do and educated. His mother recited Tagalog poetry and read Castilian prose. Rizal studied hard and did well academically, but by the time he graduated he had started to see the city, and the country, as oppressed by the colonial system. At the age of 21, seeking freedom from the friars, he set sail for Europe: the go-to destination then, before California took its place. In free-thinking Europe, he discovered a cosmopolitan world of exiles and artists, independence movements and political idealism. There too he began his first novel, *Noli Me Tangere*. Written deliberately, even provocatively, in Spanish, it was published in Germany in 1887, at his own expense, in the hope of awakening his countrymen. It is arguably the first significant anti-colonial novel by an Asian author. Rizal was then 25 and his book would change both the political future of his country and his own future.

Rizal's subversive book generated political agitation, so when he returned to the Philippines he found himself suspected of treason. He left again for Europe where he wrote his second novel, *El Filibusterismo* – a darker sequel. When he next returned to Manila, he was immediately exiled to the island of Mindanao. Four years later, he offered to go to Cuba to work as a doctor. He was allowed to set sail, but then the authorities panicked. He was brought back to Manila, charged with treason and imprisoned. On 30 December 1896, he was executed by a firing squad.

Although *Noli* is said to have provided the spark for the fight for independence from Spanish colonial rule, Rizal's preferred route appears to have been non-violent constitutional reform. A dreamer who studied ophthalmology, he sculpted, painted and wrote poetry, plays and essays as well as fiction. His last poem, *Mi Ultimo Adios*, written in his death cell, is a poignant farewell envisioning an afterlife 'where there are no slaves, tyrants or hangmen / Where faith does not kill . . .'

Contrary to Auden's claim that 'poetry makes nothing happen', things did happen as a result of that poem. Its fourteen stanzas were copied immediately after his death for family and friends, and then within months printed for the general public. They had a galvanizing effect on the independence movement. In 1902, the poem was read out in the US Congress, paving the way for autonomous government in the Philippines.

Yeats once asked, 'Did that play of mine send out / certain men the English shot?' In Rizal's case, the question is redundant. He was shot because of his words, and many others died in the course of the revolution that was inspired by his writing. But Rizal's world, despite its intimate connection with Spain, seems to have been invisible to both Auden and Yeats, as it has been to many other readers of English. It should not be so.

Noli tells the story of Crisóstomo Ibarra, a young Filipino who returns home after seven years in Europe. He is an idealist who hopes to reconnect with his roots, improve his country and marry his childhood sweetheart. Things do not go well. In Manila, he finds his father has been persecuted, and has died in prison. Crisóstomo's attempts to improve his community lead to his excommunication from the Church. His childhood sweetheart rejects him and retreats into a convent. His friends are killed. Crisóstomo ends up on the run.

It seems Rizal was looking ahead to his own return with some trepidation. *Noli* is not autobiographical, but it does foretell the trials he would face. The writing is urgent, passionate, caustic. The book opens with the announcement that Captain Tiago – a rich, land-owning liberal gentleman – is giving a dinner party in his grand Manila house.

Like an electric jolt the news circulated around the world of social parasites: the pests or dregs which God in His infinite goodness created and very fondly breeds in Manila. Some went in search of shoe polish for their boots, others for buttons and cravats, but all were preoccupied with the manner in which to greet with familiarity the master of the house, and thus pretend that they were old friends, or to make excuses, if the need arose, for not having been able to come much earlier.

You can see why the colonial class in Manila might have been upset by the book, and why Rizal was hailed as a guiding spirit by the revolutionaries who wanted to be rid of 'parasites'. No one else was writing so sharply and so mockingly in the Philippines or indeed anywhere in the colonial world in 1887 – not even his Indian contemporary Tagore.

Noli combines satire with large doses of melodrama. Rizal is youthful and earnest in exploring the political uses of fiction. But there is also a playfulness and joy in his use of language that Seamus Heaney elsewhere celebrates as the 'self-delighting inventiveness' of poetry. The issue of language lies at the heart of the novel and is used as the battleground for identity. Crisóstomo's sweetheart goes silent after refusing to marry him. Crisóstomo himself shocks his listeners by championing Tagalog. In his writing Rizal challenges the dominance of Spanish by using a Spanish peppered with Tagalog words, opening up the language in a way we tend to think of as a much more recent post-colonial phenomenon. I imagine it is a difficult book to translate but amazingly it now retains its position as the foremost Filipino novel read almost always, certainly in its homeland, in translation.

Two years ago I went back to Manila and visited Rizal's old university of Ateneo where, despite his attacks on religion, he is still regarded as their most illustrious graduate, one who apparently returned to the faith in his last moments (although the authenticity of his reaffirmation of Catholicism is fiercely disputed by some). In the Ateneo library, at last I began to read about the man known as the First Filipino. Then, with the help of Ateneo colleagues, I visited the jail in Fort Santiago where Rizal was imprisoned and followed his footsteps (inlaid in brass) to the spot where he was executed. And only now, remembering the dreams of writing I had as a boy, heading for the cool hills of Rizal province, have I come to appreciate the extraordinary achievement of *Noli*: a novel that captured a society in its pages, and then transformed it in reality.

ROMESH GUNESEKERA is the author of the Booker-shortlisted novel *Reef*. He has written eight books of fiction including *The Match*, partly set in the Philippines, and most recently *Noontide Toll*.

We have an admission to make. We've recently received a number of letters from readers complaining that they've been unable to find copies of *Tea at Florian's*, recommended by Horace Annesley of the North Eastern Gas Board in issue 56, as well as a friendly suggestion that we might reissue the book as a Slightly Foxed Edition.

So we feel it's time to come clean and confess that neither *Tea at Florian's* nor its hapless author Spencer Somers actually exists. Nor indeed does Mr Annesley – or only, that is, in the person of our regular contributor Derek Parker, who wrote the piece. He sent it to us out of the blue, it was a grey afternoon, it made us laugh and we decided to publish it as a joke for Christmas.

We hope you'll forgive us. Some of you may have raised a slightly disbelieving eyebrow when reading of Spencer's extraordinary personal history and tragic end. However, we like to think that perhaps some day, in some remote country bookshop, *Tea at Florian's* may unexpectedly come to light.

Let's Bofe

LAURA FREEMAN

When he was very young, Alan Alexander Milne fell out of a tree. He had been looking, with his brother Ken, for a toad and thought he might strike lucky up in the branches. He had already had great success with a mouse, found by his Gordon setter Brownie in a field off London's Finchley Road. This was in the 1880s when there were still fields off the Finchley Road.

Two little girls who had been playing in the field ran up. They stood hand in hand and dared each other to check that the fallen boy was all right. '*You* ask him,' said one. 'No, *you.*' Then the first said to the second: 'Let's bofe,' and together they said, 'Have you hurt yourself?' 'From then on,' Alan remembers in his autobiography *It's Too Late Now*, written when he was 59, famous and rich as a result of *Winnie-the-Pooh*, 'whenever Ken and I wanted to do a thing together we said, "Let's bofe," and giggled.'

They must have said it often. They shared beds (six holiday weeks of waking cold in the morning because the other had stolen the sheets) and baths and bikes. The bike was a tandem tricycle, which they rode up and down the Surrey hills in the summer holidays – Alan in front, Ken, being sixteen months older and stronger, behind.

At home in term-time, in the house next door to their father's boys' prep school, they would wake at five in the morning, steal down to the kitchen where Davis, the cook, kept a large bin of oatmeal, and stick their tongues in to lift a few flakes of porridge to keep

---

It's Too Late Now: The Autobiography of a Writer (1939) by A. A. Milne is out of print but we can obtain second-hand copies.

them going until breakfast proper. Thus fuelled, they would take their hoop and bowl it through the streets of London, from Mortimer Road in Kilburn all the way to the Bayswater Road and back. They were 6 and 8 at the time.

One morning, at 5.30, they took two bamboo poles, each twelve feet long, a present from their father's cousin in Jamaica, and carried them out into the playground and were Robin Hood and Will Scarlet fighting long staffs. At six o'clock, one of the masters put his head out of the window and shouted: 'What the deuce do you think you're doing?' That was the end of long staffs.

If the end of the world were to come and they were the only survivors, Alan and Ken would not have mourned. They made plans for what they would do: a dash to Kilburn High Road, darting from sweet shop to sweet shop, then across to West End Lane for marzipan potatoes, over the footbridge to the Finchley Road for jumbles – sweet ring-shaped biscuits – then up Fitzjohn's Avenue to the Heath, stopping for ice creams. 'Heaven.'

They never had a serious disagreement, but Ken mutinied once over Alan's passion for ham and eggs. On one of their country walks Alan and Ken had a 'lovely' lunch of ham and eggs. Later, they had a 'tremendous' tea of ham and eggs, and the next day a 'terrific' breakfast of ham and eggs.

> I could have gone on doing this for years, but Ken lacked something of my feeling for ham and eggs, and when at Mayfield on that second day there was nothing to be had for our midday meal but – well, as soon as he heard the unlovely words, he was (as I kindly put it) 'bilious'. So we had to go home.

When Ken bowled, Alan batted. When Ken learnt to read, he read Alan *Reynard the Fox*. When Ken was given brandy for seasickness, Alan, who had kept his composure (but only just), was given a dose too.

The great crisis of their childhood was Ken's going – curse those sixteen months – to Westminster School before Alan. They lived for the weekends when Ken came home and they bought ice creams from a shop in Brondesbury. Never has a younger brother worked so hard for his place at a school: Algebra, Euclid, Trigonometry, Geometrical Conics, Analytical Conics, Statics, Dynamics, Greek, Latin and Divinity. They were put in the same set for maths and would write on each other's books: 'SWGUSIB?' – 'Shall we go up-Sutts in break?' Up-Sutts meant 'to the tuck shop'. There they emptied their pockets and at the end of term they fiddled the accounts they showed Papa.

Much of this brought back memories. I too had been at primary school off the Finchley Road, had bought sweets on Fitzjohn's Avenue, had a bicycling younger brother who went to Westminster Under School and who stole bedclothes when forced to share on summer holidays.

I searched out *It's Too Late Now* to fill a gap. As a child I'd loved *Winnie-the-Pooh* and later I'd come across *The Enchanted Places*, a memoir by Christopher Milne – the boy who was Christopher Robin. It was sad to read of his sense of betrayal when his childhood – gingham smock, toys, bedtime prayers – was sold by his father to *Punch*. It made me curious to know more about the man who did it and why he had turned his son's childhood into fiction rather than his own.

There are certainly no forerunners of Pooh Bear in *It's Too Late Now*. Milne never mentions a favourite toy. Christopher Robin, an only child, needed the company of Piglet and Tigger and Roo and the rest. As for Milne, who needed a teddy bear when there was Ken?

And, oh, I have forgotten Barry. Poor Barry. Fifteen months older than Ken, as Ken was sixteen months older than Alan. Ken, the middle of the three sons, might have been friends with either, but it was Alan's fortune that Ken chose him.

'Whatever sort of writer I am,' observes Milne in *It's Too Late Now*, 'I am not (alas!) a "born writer".' That was Ken. But Ken, being Ken, couldn't write without wanting Alan to write with him. They signed their verse contributions to *The Elizabethan*, the Westminster school paper, 'A. K. M.' – Alan Kenneth Milne. When Ken went to be a solicitor and Alan went to Trinity College, Cambridge, to read maths, they kept it up. They honed their poems in letters back and forth and submitted them to *The Granta*, as Cambridge's *Granta* magazine was then called.

'Did you see those awfully good verses in *The Granta* this week – a new sort of limerick by somebody called A. K. M?' said the Captain of the Trinity, Cambridge football team to a 'blue' from Trinity, Oxford. Eavesdropping Alan blushed into his ginger beer. At the end of the summer term, Ken withdrew from the partnership. He wanted to write serious things for the *Cornhill* magazine, not limericks. A. K. M. became A. A. M.

Alan was made editor of *The Granta*, and R. C. Lehmann, founder and ex-editor of *Punch*, admiring the short pieces by 'A. A. M.', invited him to contribute. Ken, generous Ken, was rueful but glad.

> Whatever I did, you did a little better or a little sooner . . . And so it went on. Even after all this, I could still tell myself that I had one thing left. I should always be the writer of the family. And now you have taken that too. Well damn you, I suppose I must forgive you. My head is bloody but unbowed. I have got a new frock coat and you can go to the devil.
>
> Yours stiffly, Ken

When Alan came to London in 1903 to be a freelance writer (at first, a freelance thrower of drafts into the wastepaper basket) he took lodgings in Temple Chambers. Ken was working for the Civil Service in the Estate Duty Office and every day, at one o'clock, Alan walked up Fleet Street towards the Strand and Ken walked up from Somerset House towards Fleet Street and together they had lunch at an ABC café. When Ken married, Alan, far from being piqued or left out, took Mrs Maud Milne to his heart. She was the sister he had never had. He would go to dinner, and, to give Maud the evening off,

Alan and Ken would buy themselves the foods they'd dreamed of at Westminster: sardines, tongue, tinned fruit, cherry brandy. They cooked beef and two veg with Mrs Beeton propped on top of the oven. When Ken had his children, four in all, Alan told stories, remembered birthdays, consoled. Maud would send Christopher Robin a special pencil for Christmas with his name on it.

That was how they should have gone on all their lives. Bofe together. But here is the dedication in *It's Too Late Now*.

1880–1929

TO THE MEMORY OF KENNETH JOHN MILNE

WHO

BORE THE WORST OF ME

AND

MADE THE BEST OF ME

Only 48. Alan would live to be 74. Ken had lived his first sixteen months without Alan; Alan had twenty-seven years without Ken. In his autobiography, Milne gives 185 pages to Alan'n'Ken and their adventures; just 65 to life after Ken's death. Ken is there, doing battle with Mrs Beeton, and then suddenly he is not there. 'In the War, and afterwards, he worked himself to his death' – that is all we are told. A. A. Milne could write a thousand words for *Punch* on any subject, five times a week, could write a play, a book, a poem in an evening. But he could not write about what it was to be without Ken. Tuberculosis doesn't rhyme, grief doesn't lend itself to light verse.

Without Ken, the writing loses its bounce, the elation of the early chapters drains away. Milne rushes through his career as a journalist and playwright. His relationship with Daphne de Sélincourt, who he had married in 1913, could never fill the gap. He called her 'my collaborator', but he was only allowed to borrow her between the hairdresser and the dressmaker, and though she laughed at his jokes, they were apart for long periods of the marriage.

His attempt to make his son into another Ken was a damaging

failure. Christopher was not as gung-ho, not such a giggler, not so good at cricket. In the school holidays, Milne would take Christopher to the London ABCs where he and Ken had met for lunch. 'And when the holidays were over and I was back at school,' wrote Christopher in *The Enchanted Places*, 'his first letter to me would recall that happy lunch that he and I had had together. He and I – and the ghost of Ken . . .' Christopher felt his failings keenly: 'How nice if, when my turn came, I could have been another Ken. How sad that I wasn't.'

What we expect from Milne is lightness. Pooh carried up by his balloon. Piglet blowing dandelion seeds. Bounding Tigger. The depth of missing, of emptiness when Ken is gone from *It's Too Late Now*, comes as a shock. Deeper than the Very Deep Pit that Pooh and Piglet dig to catch a Heffalump. More desolate than Eeyore without his tail.

What can it have been like to lose a brother? No one to look for a toad. No one to fight long staffs. No one to blame for not pulling their weight on the hill climbs. No one to share ices or go up-Sutts. No letters done in rhyming couplets. No one to say: 'Let's bofe.'

LAURA FREEEMAN's first book *The Reading Cure* has just been published. Winnie-the-Pooh and his pot of HUNNY make an appearance in Chapter 7.

Out of the Celtic Twilight

ANTHONY GARDNER

A teenage boy is talking to his father in the library of their rambling Irish house. His father tells him to look at a particular picture; the moment he obeys, four armed men enter the room. But when he turns round, his father has vanished – apparently into thin air.

So, in brilliantly dramatic fashion, begins Lord Dunsany's *The Curse of the Wise Woman* (1933). As a novel it defies categorization, but if you imagine a John Buchan thriller with an overlay of the Celtic Twilight and Rachel Carson-style eco-prophecy you will be almost there. It is also a rhapsodic guide to the art of shooting wildfowl, which argues plausibly that those who wade through icy marshes with shotguns are lured by something more than bloodlust.

The main strand of the story takes place in 1885 with the narrator, Charles Peridore, on holiday from Eton. Since his mother is dead and he is an only child, his father's disappearance leaves him with just the small staff of their down-at-heel estate for company; and, anxious though he is about his father's safety, he is thrilled that he is now free to visit the nearby bog of Lisronagh in pursuit of the visiting greylag geese – 'a greater prize to me than any that the world could offer'.

The word 'bog' deserves consideration. To some people it epitomizes the supposedly primitive nature of the Irish; but anyone who has actually seen a bog will know it to be an eco-system of extraordinary complexity and – on the right day – beauty. The one at Lisronagh is to Charles 'what the desert is to an Arab', and it plays

---

Lord Dunsany, *The Curse of the Wise Woman* (1933), is out of print but we can obtain second-hand copies.

a central part in the plot. I can't think of a landscape more difficult to describe, but Dunsany manages to capture both the wonder and the danger of it:

> I walked on, under the bog's edge, with peaty soil underfoot, in which sometimes rushes grew, now all in flower, and sometimes, almost timidly, the grass . . . And all the way as I went over that quiet land there went beside me a chronicle of the ancient shudders of the Earth, old angers that had stirred and troubled the bog; for the long layers, tawny and sable, ochre, umber and orange, that were the ruins of long-decayed heather and bygone moss, went in waves all the way, sometimes heaving up into hills, the mark of some age-old uprising, sometimes cracked by clefts that sundered them twenty feet down, as though they still threatened the levels so lately stolen by man.

Charles's companion is Marlin, the gamekeeper, who knows all there is to know about birds – and about the bog, on whose edge he and his mother live. Old Mrs Marlin is an elemental figure, extraordinarily attuned to the workings of nature, and apparently able to tell the future: for, as her son eventually admits, she is a 'wise woman' – in other words, a witch.

Mrs Marlin is the self-appointed guardian of the bog, and when a peat company brings in heavy machinery to dig out the turf, Charles hopes that she may indeed have some strange power to prevent it. In the meantime, he waits for news of his father, and discovers that – as the only person who can identify the four armed men – he himself is in danger. He also falls in love with Laura, an Anglo-Irish girl who shares his fascination with the folk tales told by the Marlins about Tir-nan-Og, the land of eternal youth.

All this might make *The Curse of the Wise Woman* sound like a children's book, but it evades that category too. Charles tells the story as an old man living abroad and harking back to a vanished Ireland. The novel thus becomes a meditation on memory and the passing of time, and the skill with which Dunsany interweaves this and the other strands of the book is exemplary.

His treatment of politics is also masterful. Charles's Ireland is one in which allegiances are complex, and straight questions best avoided. The Peridores are held in high regard as gentry, sportsmen and Catholics who possess a fragment of the True Cross; but to republicans they are part of an oppressive Ascendancy, and by saving a policeman's life Charles's father is deemed to have crossed an invisible line. The leader of the gunmen sums up this ambiguity perfectly:

> There is no one we have a greater respect for than your father, but it is a pity he mixed himself up with politics the way he did; and it's the way it is we want to speak to him, and no one could be sorrier than myself that I have to say it.

Particularly fascinating is the relationship which develops between Charles and another of the gunmen, whom he comes to think of as his 'guardian demon': a figure part threatening and part protective, who has a way of materializing at unexpected moments – and who even, extraordinarily, turns to Charles for help when the police close in on him.

Dunsany, who died in 1957, is largely forgotten now, though two of his other books have cult followings – *The King of Elfland's Daughter* (which has been compared to *The Lord of the Rings*) and *My Talks with Dean Spanley* (the comic tale of a clergyman who may be the reincarnation of a dog). In his day, however, he was a considerable figure, much admired as a novelist, playwright and short-story writer. W. B. Yeats went so far as to compare his style to Baudelaire's.

For the modern reader, it is the Celtic Twilight element of *The Curse of the Wise Woman* which is hardest to accept. Marlin the gamekeeper is torn between the strictures of Christianity and the seductions of Tir-nan-Og, 'With the young men walking with the gold low light on their limbs, and the young girls with radiance on their faces, and the young blossom bursting among the apple-boughs, and all that is young there glorying in the morning'. Charles and Laura come to share his obsession; but even in the 1880s, would two educated teenagers really have given credence to such a thing?

The answer is that Yeats for one did. In his autobiographical *Reveries* he describes how, at a similar age, he wandered the Sligo countryside in search of otherworldly beings: 'I did not believe with my intellect that you could be carried away body and soul, but I believed with my emotions, and the belief of country people made that easy.'

My mother gave me *The Curse of the Wise Woman* for my fourteenth birthday, and I sometimes wonder why she chose this of all books. Did she just think it was a good read? Did she hope to spark an interest in field sports? (She herself was a keen foxhunter, and the novel contains a wonderful description of an eighteen-mile chase.) Or did she think I might identify with Charles Peridore? Like him, I divided my time between rural Ireland and an English boarding-school; I had recently lost my father; and though I didn't believe in Tir-nan-Og, I was in thrall to the Celtic Twilight and its vision of beautiful young women with pale skin and flowing hair. We were living, too, in troubled times – the 1970s – and it didn't seem impossible that we might receive a visit from armed men.

One thing we didn't have was a neighbouring bog; but that changed when my mother moved to the Knockmealdown Mountains which divide Tipperary from Waterford. The bog was small and tame compared to Dunsany's, but it was nevertheless an enchanting place – above all in summer after the rain, when sunshine turned the rivulets running through the dark peat into gleaming veins of gold. And when, in my first novel, I set about describing heaven, it was with that bog and those mountains that I began.

ANTHONY GARDNER is the author of two novels, *The Rivers of Heaven* and *Fox*. He lives in London, but visits Ireland every summer with a spaniel which may or may not be related to Dean Spanley.

Wit and Truth

ROGER HUDSON

I first delved into Lady Mary Wortley Montagu's astringent and witty letters about fifteen years ago when compiling a *Book of Days* for the Folio Society. I had to find extracts for each day of the year, written on that day – so nearly all from diaries and letters. Towards the end of my search I was left with several stubbornly blank dates, and was even thinking I might have to write bogus entries, but she, along with Pepys, as it were saved the days.

Lady Mary (1689–1762) was a creature of the Augustan Age, with an often forthright but above all rational approach to the world, far removed from the sensibility that later swept in. Lytton Strachey identified her 'outspoken clarity' – if today's social media had been around for her to use, one could see her quickly getting into trouble. She is best known for the letters she wrote from Turkey, where her husband was ambassador in 1717–18, but prior to these came the ones to him before they eloped in 1712. In those of the 1720s she told her sister of the excesses and frivolities of London society, while in the 1740s and '50s she wrote to her daughter from her self-imposed exile on the Continent.

Like Belloc's Godolphin Horne, Lady Mary was 'nobly born'; she

Robert Halsband edited the *Complete Letters* (3 vols., 1965–7). His one-volume selection was published in Britain by Penguin in 1986 but is now out of print. The definitive biography is by Isobel Grundy (1999). There are various editions of the Letters available as print-on-demand books or we can obtain second-hand copies.

might not have 'held the human race in scorn' but she often regarded it with an unblinking eye. She was the eldest child of Evelyn Pierre-pont, Earl of Kingston, later promoted Marquis and finally Duke. Her mother, a daughter of the Earl of Denbigh, died when she was only 3 and it seems likely this led to her education being 'one of the worst in the world' at the hands of a superstitious old governess who had been her mother's nurse. But she had what she called 'my natural inclinations to solitude and reading' as well as the run of her father's library, and she taught herself Latin and Greek. In the 1750s she was to offer advice about the education of her granddaughter to her daughter, Lady Bute:

> Learning (if she has a taste for it) will not only make her con-tented but happy in it. No entertainment is so cheap as reading, or any pleasure so lasting. [But] it is most absolutely necessary to conceal whatever learning she attains . . . The parade of it can only serve to draw on her the envy, and consequently the most inveterate hatred of all he and she fools, which will certainly be at least three parts in four of all her acquaintance.

From 1710 to 1712 Lady Mary's letters plot the troubled course of her relations with Edward Wortley Montagu, her eventual husband. Her best friend's brother and a grandson of 'Admiral Sandwich', Pepys's patron, he was wealthy but not prepared to agree to the marriage settlement proposed by her father, who instead touted the eligibility of an heir to an Irish viscount, worth mentioning if only for his name: Clotworthy Skeffington. But her father's objection was only part of the problem. She obviously had doubts about her own feelings, early on saying, 'I can esteem, I can be a friend, but I don't know whether I can love . . .' She also questioned Edward's ardour: 'You say you are not yet determined. Let me determine for you and save you the trouble of writing again. Adieu for ever.' A mere two months before they did finally elope she was still unremittingly realistic: 'I know you too well to propose to myself any satisfaction in marrying you that must not be centred in yourself.'

Lady Mary gave birth to a son in 1713, as well as making some criticisms of a draft of her husband's friend Addison's play, *Cato*, which became one of the century's most successful. In 1715 Edward entered Parliament, while she caught smallpox (her brother had died of it in 1713) and also attended the new Hanoverian Court. In 1716 they set out for Constantinople, calling at Vienna en route, where she was fascinated to find that

> Getting a lover is far from losing, 'tis properly getting reputation . . . It would be a downright affront and publicly resented if you invited a woman of quality to dinner without at the same time inviting her two attendants of lover and husband, between whom she always sits in state with great gravity.

But what was this, compared to the Turkish bath at Sofia? There all the ladies sat,

> without any distinction of rank by their dress, all being in the state of nature . . . I excused myself with some difficulty [from undressing]. I was at last forced to open my skirt and show them my stays, which satisfied 'em very well, for I saw they believed I was so locked up in that machine that it was not in my power to open it, which contrivance they attributed to my husband.

On the other hand,

> You may guess how effectually [their veil] disguises them, that there is no distinguishing the great lady from her slave, and 'tis impossible for the most jealous husband to know his wife when he meets her, and no man dare either touch or follow a woman in the street. This perpetual masquerade gives them entire liberty of following their inclinations without danger of discovery

... The great ladies seldom let their gallants know who they are, and 'tis so difficult to find it out that they very seldom can guess ... Those ladies that are rich have all their money in their own hands, which they take with 'em upon a divorce with an addition which [the husband] is obliged to give 'em.

She dismissed the story that the Sultan threw his handkerchief to indicate whom from his harem he selected or that she had then to 'creep in at the bed's foot', and she marvelled at the Sultana's apartments and jewels, but for posterity her most important report was of the Turks' use of inoculation against smallpox. She described the parties they held each autumn for this purpose to which old women came with nutshells 'full of the matter of the best sort of smallpox' which was then carefully inserted into children's veins with a needle. Later they would have a day or two in bed and a few scabs which left no mark. 'I am patriot enough to take pains to bring this useful invention into fashion in England.'

When home she indeed announced that her son had been inoculated in Constantinople and then her daughter in London. Caroline, the Princess of Wales, was persuaded to arrange a trial. Seven condemned prisoners were offered their freedom in return for submitting to inoculation. All survived, as did six orphans who were inoculated after them. In 1722 two of the Princess's children followed suit, and inoculation became fashionable.

It seems that by now Lady Mary's marriage was less than a bed of roses, her husband interested only in Parliament and in amassing a still larger fortune. She puzzled, 'But where are people matched! I suppose we shall all come right in Heaven, as in a country dance; though hands are strangely given and taken while we are in motion, at last all meet their partners when the jig is done.' But she could count Pope, Congreve and Gay among her friends and she took it on herself to try and raise the spirits of her sister Frances, forced into exile abroad because her husband, the Earl of Mar, the leading figure in the 1715 Jacobite rising, had been attainted. She did this with a mix of scurrilous gossip and ironical comment. Lady Bristol, 'resolved to make up for time misspent, has two lovers at a time . . . Now I think this the greatest compliment in nature to her own lord . . . being forced to take two men in his stead.' She claimed, 'There is a Bill cooking up at a hunting seat in Norfolk [Houghton, the Prime Minister Walpole's house] to have *not* taken out of the Commandments and clapped into the Creed . . . To speak plainly I am very sorry for the forlorn state of matrimony, which is as much ridiculed by our young ladies as it used to be by young fellows . . . We married women look very silly; we have nothing to excuse ourselves but that 'twas done a great while ago and we were very young when we did it.' She reported on a man who could only move one arm, in love with a woman who could not move her hands for rheumatism: 'This *amour* seems to me as curious as that between two oysters, and as well worthy the serious enquiry of the naturalists.'

It is not known why, but in 1728 Alexander Pope took against Lady Mary, referring in his *Dunciad* to some supposed financial misdoing of hers during the 1721 South Sea Bubble. His barb of 1733 was much more wounding: 'From furious Sappho scarce a milder fate, / Poxed by her love, or libell'd by her hate'. This time she gave as good as she got: 'none thy crabbed numbers can endure; / Hard as thy heart, and as thy birth obscure'. It seems this whetted her appetite, and she next took as her target one of Swift's notorious 'excremental' poems, 'The Lady's Dressing Room', which relished the disgusting details of what could be found there:

> And first a dirty smock appeared
> Beneath the armpits well besmeared . . .
> Nor be the handkerchiefs forgot
> All varnish'd o'er with snuff and snot.

Lady Mary imagined that Dean Swift had been provoked to his attack on womanhood by an unsuccessful encounter with a prostitute:

> The rev'rend lover with surprise,
> Peeps in her bubbies and her eyes,
> And kisses both and tries – and tries.

When he asks for his money back, the prostitute replies:

> What if your verses have not sold,
> Must therefore I return your gold?
> Perhaps you have no better luck in
> The knack of rhyming than of f____n'.

In 1736 the 47-year-old Lady Mary so far forgot herself as to become totally besotted with a young cosmopolitan bisexual poet and writer, Francesco Algarotti, ignoring the fact that her epicene friend Lord Hervey was equally smitten. When she set out on her travels in 1739 it was because she expected to meet him on the Continent, but this did not happen until 1741 and by then he had acquired a new and overwhelmingly powerful patron, Frederick the Great. That brought her infatuation to an end. Luckily she was able to make a new life for herself with a generous allowance from her husband: farming, gardening with advice from her son-in-law Lord Bute, later the creator of Kew, building, reading and criticizing all the latest books and observing the antics of the young English *milordi* passing through Venice or Rome on their grand tours, she herself being one of the sights to be seen. Her daughter Lady Bute dispatched boxes of novels to her from Kenwood, her Hampstead home, including those of her cousin, Henry Fielding.

In 1748 thirty local ladies and gentlemen whom she had never met before called unannounced on her at her house near Brescia in northern Italy, so she gave them a good supper and 'sent for the fiddles; they were so obliging to dance all night, and even dine with me next day, though none of them had been to bed'. The next month a gaggle of ladies dressed all in white and wearing masks arrived 'with violins and flambeaux, but did not stay more than one dance, pursuing their way to another castle'. Then the local peasants put on a sophisticated *commedia dell'arte* production for three nights in her stables.

She relished her vineyard, fish from the river, her poultry, fruit, bees and silkworms, found gardening 'certainly the next amusement to reading' and played a little whist in the afternoons. She also introduced custards, cheese-cakes, plum puddings and minced pies to her neighbours 'with universal applause', as well as the art of butter-making.

As she entered her sixties her expectations, always realistic, shaded into resignation: 'Let us be contented with our chance, and make the best of that very bad bargain of being born in this vile planet, where we may find however (God be thanked!) much to laugh at though little to approve.' The chase for worldly honours should not make people neglect 'the innocent gratification of their senses, which is all we can properly call our own'. In her reading, she told Lady Bute, 'I must be content with what I can find . . . Your youngest son is, perhaps at this very moment riding on a poker with great delight, not at all regretting that it is not a gold one, and much less wishing it an Arabian horse . . . I am reading an idle tale, not expecting wit or truth in it, and am very glad it is not metaphysics to puzzle my judgment or history to mislead my opinion.' Returning to England at last in January 1762, she died later that year.

Wit and truth are just what can be enjoyed in these letters, by a woman whose devotion to reading ought to make her some sort of exemplar for *Slightly Foxed*.

ROGER HUDSON compiled a series of books for the Folio Society in the 1990s and 2000s.

Small Player in the Great Game

AMANDA THEUNISSEN

He sat, in defiance of municipal orders, astride the gun Zam-Zammah on her brick platform opposite the old Ajaib-Gher – the Wonder House, as the natives call the Lahore Museum. Who hold Zam-Zammah . . . hold the Punjab; for the great green-bronze piece is always first of the conqueror's loot . . .

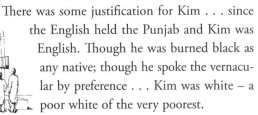

There was some justification for Kim . . . since the English held the Punjab and Kim was English. Though he was burned black as any native; though he spoke the vernacular by preference . . . Kim was white – a poor white of the very poorest.

As I read those lines the familiar magic envelops me. Kim is the eponymous hero of Rudyard Kipling's masterpiece, for many one of the best books about India ever written. It's a strange, oddly constructed book intended for children, with no proper villain, that even its author said was 'plotless' but which I have always found mesmerizing.

When I was a child, locked into the English school system, the only person I wanted to be was Kim. His life in Lahore was everything mine was not. 'Kim did nothing with an immense success . . . was hand in glove with men who led lives stranger than anything Haroun al Raschid dreamed of; and he lived a life wild as that of the

Rudyard Kipling, *Kim* (1901) · Penguin · Pb · 432pp · £8.99 · ISBN 9780141442372; Peter Hopkirk, *Quest for Kim: In Search of Kipling's Great Game* (1996) · John Murray · Pb · 288pp · £11.99 · ISBN 9780719564529

Arabian Nights, but missionaries and secretaries of charitable societies could not see the beauty of it. His nickname through the wards was "Little Friend of All the World".' Even better, I thought, he was an orphan, living his own life, unhampered by the tedious entanglements of family. He was free.

Though it was not published until 1901, Kipling wrote *Kim* in 1892, a time when the confrontation between Russia and England on the Indian North West Frontier, which he called the Great Game, was at its height. Kim – Kimball O'Hara – is a 13-year-old orphan living in Lahore. His father, a soldier in an Irish regiment, had left Kim in the care of the half-caste woman 'who pretended to keep a second-hand furniture shop by the square where the cheap cabs wait'. She was an opium addict and so Kim brought himself up on the streets, speaking English badly and thinking in Hindustani. No one knows he is a white boy, a sahib. He's intelligent, quick-witted, loyal, resourceful and brave. Able to go anywhere and pass as Muslim or Hindu, he lives by begging and by running dangerous secret errands for Mahbub Ali, an Afghan Muslim horse-trader and a spy for the English.

One day Kim befriends a Tibetan lama and, looking for adventure and new experiences, becomes the lama's disciple. Together they go on a quest: the lama is searching for the legendary Sacred River of Healing that sprang up where the Buddha's arrow fell, while Mahbub Ali gives Kim a secret package to take to a certain Colonel Creighton in Umballa – this is the boy's first, unknowing involvement in the Great Game.

Kim cares for the lama and begs for him, guarding him from 'the crows who would have picked your bones clean before you left Lahore'. By chance, they fall in with Kim's father's old regiment and the authorities determine to turn the boy into a very reluctant Christian sahib. The seemingly penniless lama pays for him to go to the best school in India. Then Mahbub Ali convinces Colonel Creighton, who turns out to be the spymaster for this part of India, that Kim would be a natural player in the Great Game. So, trained in disguise and field craft by Lurgan Sahib, the mysterious and sinister Healer of Sick Pearls in Simla, he leaves school early to go on the road with the lama again and cut his teeth in the Great Game. Eventually he and the lama get as far as the Himalayas where he and another player, a Bengali babu, foil two Russian spies.

This summary does scant justice to the book, as well as giving the impression that it is about a boy's transition from an Indian childhood to English manhood via Anglo-Indian institutions. It is, but it is also the story of a double quest – the lama for his river, Kim for himself. What gives it its unique flavour is not the action but the vivid word pictures of the characters he meets along the way and the descriptive narrative that gives an almost physical sense of actually being in India, of being part of that kaleidoscope of warmth, colour, energy, dust and smells, noise and overwhelming polyglot crowds.

Kim and the lama walk the Grand Trunk Road that traverses northern India. The lama never lifts his eyes to the throng but Kim is delighted by the sight of new people at every stride, 'castes he knew and castes that were altogether out of his experience . . . life as he would have it, bustling and shouting, the beating of bullocks and the creaking of wheels, lighting of fires and cooking of food . . . India was awake and Kim was in the middle of it.' This is India both of the imagination and of reality, even now.

The lama is forever telling Kim that 'this terrible world' is an illusion and the sooner everyone is free of it, the better. But while Kim has moments of existential doubt when he ponders who he is, white man or Indian, sahib or disciple, and where he fits into the vast universe, in the end his strength comes from being part of 'this great and beautiful land'.

There are many journeys, by train, by bullock cart or on foot, and each new place is so vividly described that you, the reader, are there too. 'Kim will remember till he dies that long and lazy journey from

Umballa up to Simla . . . the wandering road, climbing, dipping and sweeping about the growing spurs; the flush of the morning laid along the distant snows; the voices of a thousand water channels, the chatter of the monkeys, the solemn deodars climbing one after another with down-drooping branches, the vista of the plains rolled out far beneath them.' *Kim* is Kipling's love song to India, the land and the people.

Kipling has been endlessly criticized as a racist apologist for Empire. Edward Said, author of *Orientalism*, described *Kim* as 'profoundly embarrassing' and thought it an image of an exotic, obedient, changeless India invented for the pleasure of the West. Certainly no one would any longer write 'even an Oriental with an Oriental's views of the value of time' or describe Kim's astonishment that the lama 'told the truth to strangers, a thing no native would do'. Kipling was a firm supporter of Empire: in *Kim* it seems a benign institution, keeping the peace for everyone.

This was an idealized vision even then, and Kipling needed to avert his eyes from the injustice inherent in the system. However, he loved and respected the complexity of Indian life, its tolerance and warmth. *Kim* is Kipling at his most generous. Nearly all the characters are treated with affection. Even the Babu, an educated Bengali of a caste that is frequently mocked in his Indian short stories, is described with respect and admiration. This is a book where the 'native' point of view is clearly expressed, the Indian characters are more interesting than most of the European ones, and the former frequently criticize their rulers. I think this argues more tolerance and breadth of vision than Kipling is usually allowed.

The people for whom he reserved his greatest scorn and contempt were those Europeans who came to India and made no effort to understand the culture or the society, like Bennett, the Church of England chaplain of Kim's father's regiment, who looks at the lama 'with the triple-ringed uninterest of the creed that lumps nine-tenths of the world under the title of "heathen"'. Colonel Creighton warns

Kim, 'Do not at any time contemn the black men. I have known boys in the service of the Government who feigned not to understand the talk or customs of black men. Their pay was cut for ignorance. There is no sin so great as ignorance. Remember this.'

What Kipling admired in Empire was the mutual respect of ruler and ruled. On the great road Kim and the lama join forces with the elderly widow of a minor mountain rajah. They meet a white policeman who jokes with the old lady in fluent Urdu and she says, 'These be the sort to oversee justice. They know the land and the customs of the land. The others, all new from Europe, suckled by white women and learning our tongues from books, are worse than the pestilence.'

In the end, the lama finds his River of Healing by falling into an irrigation ditch in a trance, and it's clear that sooner or later Kim must choose between the exciting life of Mahbub Ali and the Great Game, the spiritual path of his guru and his role as a sahib.

In *Quest for Kim* (1996) Peter Hopkirk set out to discover as many as he could of the places Kim and the lama visit as they criss-cross the country. He also searched out the real models for the fictional characters. When Kim is learning spycraft he is taught how to measure distances using the length of his stride or by counting the beads on a rosary. He is being trained to be a 'pundit', the élite band of Indian explorers employed by the British to gather intelligence in areas too dangerous for Europeans. Add a Buddhist prayer wheel with a compass in the lid and a thermometer for calculating altitudes, and he is fully equipped. The man who thought up these ingenious gadgets and ran the 'pundits' was Colonel Thomas Montgomerie, FRS, of the Survey of India, Hopkirk's chosen candidate as the model for Colonel Creighton. Kipling had turned the real Survey of India into a fictitious India-wide intelligence service called the Ethnographical Department.

A probable match for Mahbub Ali is an actual Afghan horse-dealer of that name. Kipling knew him when he was a young journalist on the *Civil and Military Gazette* and Ali used to bring him news from untamed Afghanistan beyond the Khyber Pass. Lurgan Sahib, the sinister Healer of Pearls, is based on a real jewel merchant called A. M. Jacob (no one knows what the initials stood for) who claimed to be a Turk but might have been an Armenian or a Polish Jew. Sold into slavery as a child, he was educated by his master and rose to fame and immense wealth (according to his *Times* obituary), but he died in 1921 in poverty in Mumbai. He had a shop in Simla exactly like Lurgan Sahib's when Kipling was based there, and used to astonish everyone with his magic tricks and hypnotism.

It's fascinating to see how the real and imagined are woven together in *Kim*, but I am glad Peter never tracked down the boy himself. That leaves me free to imagine him. On my first working trip to India I filmed in the Tiger Cages, the brothels of Mumbai, and could picture Kim there, perfectly at home, teasing and laughing with the prostitutes. His world still seems very real to me, with its beggars and old soldiers, letter-writers in the bazaars, beautiful women old and young, gentle Jain monks sweeping the ground before them as they walk, merchants and a horse-trader whose thumbprint with an old diagonal scar was known from 'Balkh to Bombay'.

The world has changed since 1901 and so has India. It's a less tolerant place, but it is still full of energy, dirt, welcoming smiles and breathtaking landscapes. In my mind I can see the Little Friend of All the World embarking fearlessly on an endless journey of discovery across this vast subcontinent, merging chameleon-like into the swirling, vivid river of Indian life. Sometimes I still wish I could be Kim.

AMANDA THEUNISSEN is a television producer with a romantic streak and a hopeless, unfulfilled longing to have lived in strange, exotic places. India is top of the list.

The illustrations, by Janina Slater, are taken from Peter Hopkirk's *Quest for Kim*.

A Queer Parish

ANTHONY LONGDEN

I was on a much-rehearsed trawl of the labyrinthine bookshop when I spotted it. A neat green-cloth country volume of the type churned out in their thousands in the 1940s and '50s – years of hardship but also ones of optimism and dreams of a better future. I read the faded spine. *A House in the Country* by Ruth Adam, published by the Country Book Club, 1957.

Now this is the kind of thing I like. My bookshelves sag under the collective weight of H. J. Massingham, Adrian Bell, Ronald Blythe and Cecil Torr, but Ruth Adam was new to me. 'This is a cautionary tale, and true,' the book begins:

> Never fall in love with a house. The one we fell in love with wasn't even ours. If she had been, she would have ruined us just the same. We found out some things about her afterwards, among them what she did to that poor old parson, back in the eighteen-seventies. If we had found them out earlier . . . ? It wouldn't have made any difference. We were in that maudlin state when reasonable argument is quite useless. Our old parents tried it. We wouldn't listen. 'If you could only *see* her,' we said.

As the Second World War draws to a close, a group of six friends pool resources in order to rent a sizeable House in the Country – capital H, capital C. Their list of requirements is exacting. It has to be 'one of those houses that's been built bit by bit, for hundreds of

---

Ruth Adam, *A House in the Country* (1957), is out of print but we can try to obtain second-hand copies.

Claire Dalby, 'Nettlecome: Garden in October', wood engraving, 55 x 68mm

years'. It has to have acres of land and dozens of outhouses. As it turns out, such a house does exist, a pretty, rambling but rather run-down Tudor manor house in deepest Kent. And so they move in.

Adam's gentle, witty and compelling story is peopled by many memorable characters, especially old Howard, the gardener and general factotum. He had been with the old colonel, the manor's late owner, since he was a pageboy in buttons, and he is the beating heart of the place, its wily and loyal retainer.

The colonel had a daughter, and it isn't long before she asserts herself, albeit from a distance. Howard brings bad news: the refrigerator in the kitchen doesn't belong to the house at all – the colonel gave it to her before he died and now she wants it back. That is just the beginning:

> 'Those fire extinguishers,' said Howard, a few days later. 'She couldn't understand why those had been left for you. It seems she had some arrangement with the colonel about them.'

A large area of linoleum follows suit, and the colonel's daughter even lays claim to the Cox's apple trees that Howard had previously told Adam were the best in the entire garden.

Predictably enough, the adjustment from town to country is anything but smooth, and I love the way in which Adam nibbles away at the friends' collective dream, steadily eroding it as the book progresses. They are still settling in when the vicar calls:

'I'm afraid you'll find the parishioners an undesirable collection on the whole,' he said. 'It's a queer parish, very. I only took it because the last man didn't like flying bombs and asked me to exchange. But since I've come here, I've wondered if he was deceiving me and that it wasn't the flying bombs he minded. I should advise you very strongly to steer clear of the policeman. He's a very queer chap indeed. However, I expect the authorities will find him out before long.'

A few days later there is another knock at the door. It is the policeman.

He was young and extremely handsome and rather public school. 'Natives are a rum lot,' he said. 'I've had to set the young chaps on slave labour, building themselves a club, to get the place under control. Remind me to show you over some time.'

Various neighbours and interlopers turn out to have arcane and often inconvenient rights of access or storage. A farmer keeps all his harrows, tractors, hay-carts and bits of harvester in the outbuildings. A mysterious man in a bowler hat walks up and down the drive to a cottage in the grounds without ever saying a word to anyone. And there are other puzzling encounters.

One day, there were three men standing knee deep in the river. They wished me good morning as I went by. Later on, I found them cutting down a tree and thought this was pressing hospitality too far. 'There's nothing you can do,' said Howard when I found him. 'They got a right to do anything at all they like. They're the Kent Catchment Board.'

Howard is, however, getting tired. He complains that the garden is becoming too much for him, and places most of the blame at the door of the Americans, claiming that the dropping of the atom bomb has altered the weather and skewed the seasons to such an extent he can no longer keep up. When he eventually says he is going to give up altogether, the friends are devastated:

> We felt the bottom had dropped out of our world. It was not only that Howard could cope with every emergency. There was something more important than that. It was Howard who had been our essential link with the past. He had taught us to understand the way the machinery of the great house and garden worked . . . We tried to imagine running the manor without Howard. It was impossible.

The inevitable happens. Howard, whose world is contracting around him, is on the threshold of his final illness, and although arrangements are made to keep things running with the help of two younger men from the village, the die is cast.

Adam is the keenest and often most touching of observers. Here is her description of Howard's passing:

> Twice every day I called at the cottage to ask how he was. I would hear her slow, heavy footsteps painfully descending the narrow stairs. When she at last reached the door and opened it, she was speechless and panting for breath. One day, I could not bear to fetch her struggling down again, and decided that my inquiry was more trouble to her than it was worth. I got as far as the stable yard and turned back. Howard died that evening.
>
> 'He kept on asking for you,' the old wife said without reproach. 'I said – "She's sure to call in to inquire, like she always does, and then I'll ask her if she'll kindly step upstairs for a chat."'
>
> Even at this distance of time, I remember the lilacs heavy with rain and the cuckoo calling mournfully, as I went back up through the garden. It taught me one lesson for life – when in

doubt, always make your gesture. The risk of being a nuisance is the lesser one.

The friends never really recover from this blow. After several years, and in light of experience, they go their separate ways, having had enough of their communal countryside experiment. After all, as Sartre said, 'Hell is other people.'

*

A vicar's daughter, Ruth Adam was born Ruth King in Arnold, Nottinghamshire, in December 1907. After attending boarding-school in Derbyshire, she was plunged into the grime and poverty of Nottingham's mining villages, where she worked as a teacher. In 1932 she married Kenneth Adam, then a journalist on the *Manchester Guardian* but who later rose to become the BBC's Director of Television. The couple had three sons and one daughter.

Adam moved from teaching into writing, and her work – be it novels (she wrote twelve of them), radio scripts for *Woman's Hour*, social commentary or journalism – had a strong feminist theme running through it. She worked for the Ministry of Information during the war, wrote the women's page for the *Church of England Newspaper* from 1944 to 1976, and even produced comic strips in *Girl* magazine, launched in 1951, creating a number of strong female characters who were independent-minded and resourceful. Perhaps her best-known work is *A Woman's Place*, a polemic challenge to male chauvinism, and a world away from *A House in the Country*. She died on 3 February 1977 in London at the age of 69.

So was *A House in the Country*, with all its charm and insight, fact or fiction? As with that great country chronicler, S. L. Bensusan (*SF* no. 41), the answer is probably a bit of both, but the result is tender and genuine.

ANTHONY LONGDEN is a freelance journalist and a specialist partner at a crisis-handling firm. He is fighting a losing – and frankly half-hearted – battle against a steadily rising tide of books that threatens to engulf his home.

Making Manifest

RICHARD HOLLOWAY

The American philosopher Arthur Danto described the human animal as an *ens representans*, a being that represents the world back to itself. And we can't help doing it. Give a small girl a crayon and a sheet of paper and she'll draw her mummy and daddy and the cat on the mat before the fireplace. Listen to people on the bus going home from work and they'll be telling their day over again to their friends. All the glories of human art and creativity flow from this compulsion to represent or describe or call back all the worlds we experience. And some have the capacity for representing the world to an almost miraculous degree. We call them artists and we say of them what Beckett said of Joyce, that what he wrote was not *about* something, it was *that something itself*. Great art makes its subject so manifest that we can enter and experience it for ourselves. And sometimes it breaks the heart.

I have been breaking my heart over and over again by a constant reading of a novel that is a distillation of the world's sorrow. I read it first when I was a 44-year-old priest facing another Good Friday with nothing left to say. Suffering is the dilemma that confronts the honest preacher on Good Friday. Suffering and *God!* For how do they go together? Whatever direction you take you hit a wall. If there is no God, what becomes of all that pain? But if God does exist, how can he endure the sorrow of a single child?

That's the anguish I was wrestling with in 1977 when I picked up

---

We can try to obtain second-hand copies of the English edition of André Schwarz-Bart, *The Last of the Just* (1959).

The Last of the Just by André Schwarz-Bart. It had won the Prix Goncourt when it was published in France in 1959, but this was the Penguin Modern Classics edition, translated by Stephen Becker. Reading it changed how I thought about suffering. Not because it solved the dilemma I was wrestling with, but because it *expressed* it to an unbearable degree. It proved to me that the work of the preacher, like the work of the artist, was not to explain but to reveal. Not to *tell* but to *show*. Schwarz-Bart's novel was not *about* the Holocaust. It *was* the Holocaust. And to read it was to enter not only the ancient travail of the Jews, but also the depthless cruelty of the so-called religion of love that had caused it.

Like Jews everywhere for the last two thousand years, the Schwarz-Bart family had kept their suitcases packed ready for the next expulsion. In 1924 they moved from Poland to France – where André was born in 1928 – in order to keep ahead of the terror that was stirring. But it caught up with them in 1941 when André's parents and two brothers were deported to Auschwitz and died there. Alone in the world at 15, André evaded capture, joined the French Resistance and fought back against the horror that had engulfed his people. He survived the war and died in Guadeloupe in 2006. Like Harper Lee of *To Kill a Mockingbird*, he is remembered for a single novel – maybe because to write such a moral and artistic masterpiece exhausts the resources of the creator. And in *The Last of the Just* he distilled a thousand years of Jewish suffering into a single fiction.

Beginning with a pogrom in York in the twelfth century, he follows the story of thirty-six Just Men of Jewish legend. He tells us:

According to this tradition the world reposes upon thirty-six Just Men, the *Lamed-waf*, indistinguishable from simple mortals; often they do not recognize themselves. But if even one of them were lacking, the sufferings of mankind would poison even the souls of the new-born, and humanity would suffocate with a single cry. For the *Lamed-waf* are the hearts of the world multiplied, into which all our griefs are poured, as into one receptacle.

The last of the Just Men is Ernie Levy, who is delivered to Auschwitz in 1943 with his betrothed, Golda, and a band of children he has been protecting. In the final scene they are taken to a huge bath-house where they are met by a moustached and apparently benevolent member of the SS. He tells them that nothing painful is going to happen to them. But they have to be disinfected to prevent contagious diseases. He points to the coat hooks along the wall on which they are to hang their clothes. Each of them has a number. Remember your number, he tells them, so you can reclaim your clothes when you've had your shower. Then they are given cakes of stony soap and told to strip.

Golda begged Ernie not to look at her, and he went through the sliding door of the second room with his eyes closed, led by the young woman, and by the children, whose soft hands clung to his naked thigh; there, under the shower-heads embedded in the ceiling, in the blue light of screened bulbs glowing in the recesses of the concrete walls, Jewish men and women, children and patriarchs, were huddled together; his eyes still closed, he felt the pressure of the last packets of flesh that the SS men were clubbing now into the gas chamber; and his eyes still closed, he knew that the lights had been extinguished on the living . . . And when the first waves of 'Zyklon B' gas billowed among the sweating bodies, drifting towards the squirming carpet of children's heads, Ernie freed himself from the girl's mute embrace and leaned out into the darkness towards the children invisible even at his knees, and shouted, with all the gentleness and all the strength of his soul, 'Breathe deeply, my lambs, and quickly!'

When I first read those words I paused, and again the old question asserted itself. Where was God when the Zyklon B gas drifted down on that squirming carpet of children's heads? That was the doubt Good Friday always raised in me. And here it was again. None of the theologians I had read answered it or even seemed to understand the anger that prompted it. They blamed it on free will. God loved us so much that he had renounced his power to compel us and had given us freedom to use well or badly. Though it broke his heart to see how constantly we abused it, he would not revoke his dangerous gift. But in the end we would understand how necessary all that pain was and all would be well again. Thus spake the theologians. And Ivan Karamazov in another great novel flattened them like a house of cards.

> Imagine that you yourself are building the edifice of human destiny with the object of making people happy in the finale, of giving them peace and rest at the last, but for that you must inevitably and unavoidably torture just one tiny creature, that same child who was beating her chest with her little fist, and you raise your edifice on the foundation of her unrequited tears – would you agree to be architect on such conditions?
>
> And can you admit the idea that the people for whom you are building would agree to accept their happiness on the unjustified blood of a tortured child, and having accepted it, to remain forever happy?

Like Ivan Karamazov, André Schwarz-Bart rejected the God of the theologians. But he also knew it left the great question unanswered:

> If God did not exist . . . he wondered, where does all the suffering go? And . . . he cried out, in a sob that ripped through the darkness of the workshop: *It gets lost, oh my God, it gets lost!*

Except that in his novel the suffering was not lost. It was given a voice. And as the gas descended it spoke into the silence of God:

> first as a stream, then a cascade, then an irrepressible, majestic

torrent, the poem which, through the smoke of fires and above the funeral pyres of history, the Jews – who for two thousand years never bore arms and never had either missionary empires or coloured slaves – the old love poem which the Jews traced in letters of blood on the earth's hard crust unfurled in the gas chamber, surrounded it, dominated its dark, abysmal sneer . . . SHEMA ISRAEL ADONAI ELOHENU ADONAI EH'OTH . . . Hear O Israel, the Eternal our God, the Eternal is One.

The gift André Schwarz-Bart gave me as a preacher trying to address the world's endless Good Friday was to recognize that though the Church's official theology would rarely help me, good art always would. And it was W. H. Auden who showed me why. He expressed it in his poem on the death of W. B. Yeats.

> . . . Mad Ireland hurt you into poetry.
> Now Ireland has her madness and her weather still,
> For poetry makes nothing happen: it survives
> In the valley of its making . . .
> A way of happening, a mouth.

Like poetry, honest preaching may make nothing happen, but it can give pain a mouth. It can bear witness; give testimony; set the truth down.

In the chapel in the Garden of Gethsemane in Jerusalem there used to be a sign aimed at tour guides who broke the silence of that place of sorrow. NO EXPLANATIONS IN CHURCH. It's still the best advice.

RICHARD HOLLOWAY's new book, *Waiting for the Last Bus*, is published by Canongate.

Dere Diary . . .

PETER PARKER

In October 1881 a 14-year-old London schoolboy called Ernest Baker started keeping a diary. 'In this little book I intend to give a full and faithful account of the remarkable events of my life,' he announced, 'although of course my life is no more remarkable than anyone else's life but however I hope it may interest some one.'

What I want from a diary is not necessarily remarkable events, but a vivid sense of the author's character and of the times in which he or she lived. Though it covers a mere four months, Ernest Baker's diary more than satisfies this requirement, providing a marvellous picture of everyday life in Shoreditch in the early 1880s filtered through the consciousness of a lively and irreverent adolescent.

Ernest had been given the diary by 'his dear Papa', the Reverend Henry Baker, who as Chaplain to the Ironmonger's Company had charge of the Geffrye Almshouses in London's East End. The almshouses were home to some fifty or so women pensioners with connections to the Ironmonger's Company – or, as Ernest characteristically put it, 'old biddies, who are resting the remains of their shattered lives in these grounds'. The Chaplain lived with his large family on the premises, took services in the chapel, supervised the staff and attended to both the spiritual and physical welfare of the pensioners. The almshouses are now the home of the Geffrye Museum, to which the diary was left by one of Ernest's nieces in 1988 and by which it was published the following year as *A Victorian Schoolboy in London*.

David Rogers (ed.), *A Victorian Schoolboy in London: The Diary of Ernest Baker, 1881–1882* (Geffrye Museum, 1989), is out of print.

Ernest Edward Baker was born on 9 November 1866, the sixth of the Reverend Baker's nine children. At the time he was writing his diary, he was attending a crammer in Cannon Street run by a Dr Julius Klein. 'I having a strong desire to go into the army am sent there to be prepared for the Sandhurst military college examination,' Ernest explains in the first entry in his diary, dated 10 October 1881. Also enrolled at Klein's was his brother Septimus (Seppy), who was 13 and Ernest's closest companion.

The regime at Klein's seems to have been fairly relaxed – pupils arrived at 11 a.m., had an hour off for lunch, and usually set off home again at 4 p.m. – and Ernest's family recall that he was far more interested in mucking about than in attending to his studies. He was apparently the favourite among his siblings because he was so funny, quick-witted and easygoing, and these qualities come across in the diary, which he illustrated with his scratchy and highly amusing little drawings.

It seems probable that Ernest had been given the diary with the idea that writing in it would be a good daily discipline. It may also have been hoped that this exercise would improve his spelling and punctuation, which at times give Nigel Molesworth a run for his orthographical money (and have sensibly been left uncorrected in the published edition). 'These last few days dear reader I must acknowledge with many apoligies that I have been writing very thick and sluvenly,' he confesses at one point, adding that 'bad spelling . . . is a defect I try to overcome, strange to say but true, that the Bakerians naturally spell very well, I am afraid I must add with many a bitter but false tear that I am an exception.' This gives a good flavour both of Ernest's style and his irresistible bumptiousness.

The diary's earlier entries tend to be quite short, as if Ernest were indeed fulfilling a daily duty; but after taking a month off, he returns to the task at Christmas 1881 with new energy, writing at greater length and in more detail. He even acknowledges where entries have fallen short: 'This day's diary has been hurried over a little on account of violent headache caused by tumpling down stairs,' he apologizes on 11 January 1882. Although he writes a good deal about his recreations – keeping hens, constructing a highly dangerous swing-cum-battering-ram from scaffolding poles, brandishing real swords while playing with Seppy – Ernest is also very informative about food, furniture, shopping and family celebrations. We discover what a middle-class Victorian paterfamilias might expect from his children on his birthday (pens, blotters, ink, a box of rubber bands, a corkscrew, a 'transparent shaving stick' and, from Ernest, 'a little candlestick'); that although the family ate goose on Christmas Day, stockings and presents were opened, and plum pudding consumed, on Boxing Day; and how much time everyone spent going to a wide variety of shops, both locally and further afield, in search of such useful items as sou'westers and a sausage-making machine.

The children regularly attend daunting-sounding lectures: 'The routes of trade and commerce in Prehistoric Europe', 'The cause and phenomina [*sic*] of dreams', 'The essay in the nineteenth century'. This last left Ernest with the impression that 'Montaine' was 'the first essayist . . . and must have lived about 400 years ago, perhaps at the time of "Euclid"' – which makes one wonder about the quality of education offered at Dr Klein's establishment.

David Rogers, who has done an excellent job of introducing and annotating the diary for publication, finds Ernest immature by today's standards, but also rightly says that modern sensibilities should not be brought to bear on the antics of a Victorian schoolboy.

Ernest and Seppy regularly consume wine and wander round London with a freedom and self-sufficiency unimaginable today for boys of their age. Ernest also writes casually about spending time with 'an idiot boy', who cannot join in cricket and football 'on account of his legs bending in at the ankles'; conducts a rather drastic experiment to ascertain whether or not a tortoise is still alive; and goes to inspect the corpse of one of the pensioners: 'I uncovered it as far as its head, I pinched its cheek and found it cold, I lifted its head up and found it was heavy, I turned its head round, and found it wouldn't go; I went out.' This dispassionate account, as much as his fondness for excruciating puns and terrible jokes (think *The Diary of a Nobody*), reminds us that Ernest was very much of his time. He was also no respecter of persons, and freely criticizes his elders and betters: incompetent teachers, squalling concert musicians, 'that unimaginable little beast Klein', and a 'muffin faced young man' who drops in on the family unannounced. Reprimanded by a librarian for his bad behaviour during a lecture, he writes airily: 'I only laughed that a mere "bookduster" was trying to have authority.'

Like many boys of his age, Ernest is conscious of his appearance, often returning clothes to retailers for a better fit. He records one terrible occasion when a game of charades at the home of some family friends becomes an ordeal 'on account of a tare I had at the back of my trousers', which his Eton 'bum freezer' jacket fails to conceal. He explains that he hadn't changed into smarter clothes because he thought he was merely dropping in to bring his sisters home; asked to stay, he'd been obliged to remove his overcoat, which had 'covered everything'.

In spite of his generally anarchic behaviour, Ernest is capable of standing on his dignity – often with unintentionally comic results. On one occasion he unsuccessfully attempts to persuade a policeman to arrest a drunken woman who has 'insulted' him in the fogbound streets. (The woman, perhaps not entirely without provocation, had given him a smart clip round the ear.)

The last page of the diary announces: 'A second but thinner DIARY will be commenced in a weeks time, and will go by the name of Vol: II being a supplement to this DIARY.' This promise, alas, remained unfulfilled, and the rest of the story is told by Ernest's youngest sister Lena in a short unpublished family memoir also donated to the Geffrye Museum, who kindly provided me with a copy. Readers will not be wholly surprised to learn that Ernest failed his Sandhurst entrance exams. To his parents' dismay, he instead enlisted as a ranker in the 15th Hussars. They bought him out and found him a job as a commercial clerk, but after a short time he arrived home to say that he had once again enlisted as a private and would be sailing with his regiment to India in a couple of days' time. He would die there in 1892 after being thrown against a wall by his bolting horse. He was just 25 and is buried in Muttra in West Bengal.

Lena writes that Seppy had followed his oldest brother Hal into the Merchant Navy and was lost at sea on his second voyage. A bit of research led me to discover that in 1884 he had signed a four-year apprenticeship aboard the *Berwick Law*, which on 19 March 1886 set sail from what was then Akyab in Burma and was never heard of again. He was 18. It is a heart-breaking end for the two carefree boys we left in February 1882 playing at 'cutting oranges with swords'; but there is a further coda. Quite by chance I discovered that Seppy had also kept a diary, in which he recorded his first year at sea. It is now in the library of the National Maritime Museum at Greenwich, and provides a detailed account of life aboard a Victorian merchant vessel. No one seems to have spotted the family connection between these two juvenile diaries, but it would be nice to see them published together, perhaps with Lena's memoir to make the story complete.

PETER PARKER has written biographies of J. R. Ackerley and Christopher Isherwood and two books about those who fought in the First World War. His most recent book, *Housman Country*, is a cultural history of *A Shropshire Lad*.

A Tasmanian Tragedy

PENELOPE LIVELY

Matthew Kneale's *English Passengers* (2000) has to be called a historical novel; it is set in 1857. Now, I have a resistance to the historical novel, but this writer is one of those, along with J. G. Farrell and John Fowles, who redeem the genre for me. The book was a prize-winner when it was published in 2000 but I feel it may be undeservedly overlooked today, perhaps because Matthew Kneale is a costive writer, with only a couple of other novels appearing since. To compensate for that, *English Passengers* is a masterpiece, an achievement of such complexity, ingenuity and sheer narrative power that each time I reread it I am newly surprised: how can a writer have thus conjured up the wildly conflicting attitudes of another time, another place, with such persuasive force?

This is an instance of what is called the multi-voice novel – in spades. There are various voices – fifteen or more – but a small handful of crucial ones power the story. Three mid-Victorian gentlemen have chartered a ship crewed by Manxmen with the purpose of sailing to Tasmania. Two of them are obsessive to the point of mania: the Reverend Geoffrey Wilson is convinced that Tasmania is where the actual site of the Garden of Eden can be found; Dr Potter, a surgeon, has a sinister and perverted interest in racial types. The third member of the party, Timothy Renshaw, is a young botanist, propelled by his father to join the expedition in the belief that it will be a character-building experience.

Matthew Kneale, *English Passengers* (2000)
Penguin · Pb · 480pp · £8.99 · ISBN 9780140285215

Then there is Illiam Quillian Kewley, captain of the *Sincerity*, which is in fact – unknown to those who have chartered the ship – a smuggling vessel, with a cargo of brandy and tobacco hidden aboard. And, most crucially of all, there is the voice of Peevay, a Tasmanian aboriginal boy. Peevay's mother was abducted and raped by an escaped convict turned seal-hunter. We learn of this event from Jack Harp, the rapist, and of how the woman escaped. She becomes the leader of an aboriginal group, and for the rest of her life is fired by bitter hatred of Europeans and a mission to find and kill her rapist. Interestingly, her voice is never heard – we see her entirely through the eyes of her son, whom she despises and rejects on account of his parentage.

As the story unfolds, more voices are added – those of the colonizers who are occupying the island and setting about the systematic obliteration of the way of life of its native inhabitants and, in due course, the inhabitants themselves. There are conflicting attitudes here. Many of the settlers are former convicts, who simply slaughter parties of aborigines whenever they come across them. The Governor, finding the colony more or less ungovernable, feels impelled to set the militia on native raiders in order to appease the more vocal colonists, and is seeking to move the entire surviving aboriginal population to one corner of the island, away from their traditional hunting grounds.

This multi-voice technique is the perfect – perhaps the only – way in which to present this terrible apposition of inhumanity and a kind of innocence. Though it would be wrong to regard the aborigines as complete innocents: they are accustomed to pretty brisk treatment of one another in tribal warfare, and are indeed capable of the killing of settlers, of which they are accused. But they are innocent of the sophistry whereby the Governor, and indeed pretty well everyone else, can justify their eviction from their ancestral homelands simply because their presence is an inconvenience. The aborigines don't understand, at first, what is going on. When eventually they do, it is too late.

Alongside the story of Peevay and his group, there is the parallel story of the *Sincerity*, her crew and the maniacal Reverend Geoffrey Wilson and Dr Potter. There is wry humour here, in the plight of Captain Kewley, who had never intended to sail round the world but was simply involved in a traditional Manx smuggling operation, for which his ship had been specially kitted out, with hidden compartments. But everything goes wrong at the outset, and he is obliged to masquerade as a charter vessel; intending to dump his charterers when that becomes expedient, he is unable to do so, and finds himself on the way to Tasmania.

Throughout, voice succeeds voice. We skip from the Reverend Geoffrey Wilson's sanctimonious version of events to Dr Potter's pseudo-scientific ravings, from Captain Kewley's opportunism to Peevay's stoical but bewildered account of tribal wanderings.

There are two narratives, effectively, and the skill of the storytelling is such that, in the end, the two meld into one, and the story of Peevay and his mother, with her furious intent on revenge, elides with that of the increasingly demented Victorian adventurers.

Matthew Kneale includes an epilogue in which he says that the major events of the Tasmanian strand of the story are based on historical fact: the massacre of aborigines and subsequent isolation of the survivors on Flinders Island, with even the character of Peevay's mother echoing that of a formidable aborigine woman who attempted to fight back against the settlers. Most of us, I think, have some idea of the Tasmanian saga anyway, but the reason Kneale is so persuasive as a historical novelist is that he writes without leaving the reader with any sense of the research that underlies the book; it is invisible, like the seven-eighths of an iceberg without which it would capsize. He has managed to become a ventriloquist, imbuing the narrative with all the requisite conflicting attitudes and motivations: the mindless brutality of those running the convict barracks at Port Arthur, the insensitive pieties of those seeking to indoctrinate the surviving – and dying – aborigines with Christian virtues, the bizarre lunacy of the Reverend Geoffrey Wilson in his pursuit of the Garden of Eden.

A fine irony here, of course. If anywhere is the antithesis of the Garden of Eden, it is Tasmania in the mid-nineteenth century, site of one of the most effective ethnic cleansings ever. The calamitous expedition into the bush to find the site, led by Peevay himself, is wonderfully described from the points of view of a group entirely at odds with one another – Wilson effectively crazy, Peevay with his own agenda – while the impervious landscape serves as a backdrop that is about as far from an Eden as it is possible to get. And then, when the reader feels that this has to be the climax, there comes the startling coda of the journey back to England, when fortunes are reversed and Captain Kewley and his crew are made captives in their own ship. The ending is unexpected, and entirely appropriate.

It is the success of the multi-voice technique that, for me, overcomes my problem with the historical novel. *English Passengers* makes me forget that that is what I am reading. There is no authorial voice, no detached narrative, the past is made to speak for itself, to speak in many voices, and because Kneale is so skilled with a technique that would floor most writers, an almost unimaginable time and place come alive. Actually, his choice of subject is ideal: Tasmania at that point serves up such an ill-assorted populace that wildly conflicting viewpoints are inevitable. Settlers, convicts, militia, those attempting to impose order and the evasive, inscrutable aborigines are all at odds with one another in a way that makes for a perfect demonstration of what would today be called an underdeveloped society. Eventually, of course, Tasmania will become viable, but at extraordinary expense, with the most extreme victims those who never wanted to be there at all – the convicts – and those from whom it was commandeered – the aborigines.

Before I end I should declare an interest. I met Matthew Kneale in Australia, back in the 1980s, at the Adelaide Literary Festival. He was in his late twenties; I had enjoyed his first novel and was glad to hear that his publishers had asked the festival organizers if he could join the British contingent since he was on a trip to Tasmania anyway. The festival had a most civilized practice of sending the long-haul writers – the Brits and the Americans – to unwind before the festival for a few days at an idyllic motel in the vineyard country outside Adelaide, and Matthew met up with us there. He blew in, every inch the hardened travelling writer, in shorts, bush hat, backpack, very evidently fresh from the bush, and putting us to shame with our jet-lag and our luggage (Marilyn French with a set of five matching cases including a hatbox). He was good company. And I now realize that he must at that time have been incubating *English Passengers*.

PENELOPE LIVELY will never get to Tasmania or write a historical novel, but she reads history all the time, and enjoys vicarious travel by way of television documentaries.

High Society, Low Life

ANTHONY WELLS

Marcel Proust's novel *Remembrance of Things Past* begins, as I discussed in an earlier piece (*SF* no. 56), with the narrator recalling the
times he spent as a boy in his great-aunt's house in the village of
Combray. There were two walks the family regularly took from the
house, one in the direction of a property owned by a family friend,
M. Swann, and the other in the direction of an estate owned by a
very grand aristocratic family with local connections, the Guermantes.
The Way by Swann's, the first walk, is the name of the first book of
Proust's novel. *The Guermantes Way*, the second walk, is the name of
the third, and with it the narrator and reader enter a new world, of
dukes and duchesses, princes and princesses, and all the high society
of Paris's fashionable Faubourg Saint-Germain.

The narrator's knowledge of the Guermantes, as with almost
everything else in Proust's vast but subtly constructed work, begins at
a very early stage. They appear first in the form of a medieval ances-
tor, Geneviève de Brabant, in the magic-lantern slides projected on
to the curtains of the young boy's Combray bedroom. Another ances-
tor of this ancient French family is present in the local church, where
Gilbert the Bad, a descendant of Geneviève, is depicted in one of the
stained-glass windows. As a result, the name Guermantes is wrapped
in mystery for the young boy, associated as it is with the remotest

The first English translation, by C. K. Scott Moncrieff, is available from
Vintage in six paperbacks. It is also available in hardback, in a four-volume
boxed set, from Everyman at £65 (ISBN 9781857152500). A new translation by
several hands is available from Penguin, also in six paperbacks.

medieval past and with maidens awaiting rescue in the bedtime story read to him by his great-aunt. So when one day he catches a glimpse of the Duchesse de Guermantes in the flesh, at a wedding in the church where she is a guest of honour, he is disappointed to find that she looks little different from other women he knows, 'a fair-haired lady with . . . a pimple at the corner of her nose'.

We step into the world of the Guermantes proper, however, when the narrator – now an adolescent – and his family move to their new apartment in Paris, in a wing of the Guermantes' residence. The move takes place at the beginning of *The Guermantes Way* and here and in

the succeeding book, *Sodom and Gomorrah*, we find ourselves in the brilliant (and not so brilliant) social world of the salons, a seemingly endless round of afternoon and evening receptions, gala opera perform-ances and glittering lunches and dinners, from select gatherings at the Duchesse de Guermantes' to a less select five o'clock tea at Mme Swann's or a musical evening at the wealthy but pedigreeless Mme Verdurin's (where the love affair between Swann and his mistress Odette is played out).

There are seven major parties of one kind or another in the course of *Remembrance of Things Past*, and they occupy in all 750 pages of the 3,000-page novel; if we included the smaller functions, a lunch at Mme Swann's where the narrator meets his writer hero Bergotte, or the evening reception where Swann, hearing again the bewitching little phrase from the sonata by the composer Vinteuil, realizes his love for Odette is dead, the page count would be nearer one-third of the entire work.

The life of the salons and their hostesses and regular guests, the finely graded relations between the different layers of the *gratin*, the upper crust, furnish the human raw material of Proust's (fictional) history of his times. These salons are not the arena of action, of political negotiation and decision-making: the movers and shakers of contemporary events – Marshal MacMahon and General Boulanger, Kaiser Wilhelm and Clemenceau, Alfred Dreyfus, his defender Zola and the Army High Command – remain in the wings, mentioned only in conversation, or in connection with lesser-known relatives, or (as in the case of Dreyfus) as a cause of ruptured friendships, social disapproval or ostracism. The events that agitated the France of those decades – the Panama corruption scandal of the 1890s, the Dreyfus Affair, the Moroccan crisis of 1905, and not least the Great War – are visible only in the background, filtered through the personalities and attitudes, reactions and words of this privileged, distinguished, stylish, callous and ultimately (in the narrator's view) vacuous social stratum.

At the outset, though, the narrator is starstruck by the brilliance of this world, presided over by its wittiest and most elegant hostess, Oriane, Duchesse de Guermantes. Through his friendship with the duchess's nephew, the narrator gains his longed-for introduction to her; he now has his entrée into high society. What he finds there provides the material for a comedy of manners on the grand scale, and permits Proust, through a huge cast of characters from every level of salon life, to display the vanity, egotism, ambition, snobbery and enslavement to fashion of these privileged creatures, which he does with a mordant wit reminiscent of the *Maxims* of La Rochefoucauld. (Proust's model for his portrayal of these latter-day kingless courtiers was a contemporary of La Rochefoucauld's, the Duc de Saint-Simon, whose memoirs had provided just such a sharp and witty portrait of the court of Louis XIV.)

The sharpest lens through which the attitudes and behaviour of these titled and moneyed glitterati are examined is the Dreyfus Affair which, during the 1890s, split not just the French upper classes but the whole of French society into two separate camps, centred on the court martial of a Jewish officer, Captain Alfred Dreyfus, for passing military secrets to the Germans, and the campaign to prove his innocence. The Affair weaves in and out of the salon conversations, highlighting the mechanisms by which individuals and social groups coalesce around certain views – not at all for identical reasons, or for necessarily honourable motives – and then change their minds, perhaps because the facts have changed, perhaps simply not to seem out of step. The Duc de Guermantes is a case in point. Here he is commenting on the risk to his nephew Robert de Saint-Loup's membership of the most exclusive club in Paris posed by his support for Dreyfus:

> 'But,' he went on in a gentler tone, 'you'd be the first to admit that if one of our family were to be refused membership of the Jockey, especially Robert, whose father was president for ten years, it would be an outrage . . . Personally, I have no racial prejudice, you know that. That sort of thing is very out of date to me, and I like to be thought of as moving with the times. But God damn it! With a name like the Marquis de Saint-Loup, one isn't a Dreyfusard. And that's all there is to it.'

Never mind whether Dreyfus is innocent or not, it is the family name that counts. Later on, however, we learn that the duke has entirely reversed his views, not because of the merits of the case but because, during a visit to a spa, an Italian princess had told him that 'nobody with a grain of intelligence can ever have believed for a moment' that there was any evidence against Dreyfus.

Swann's shifting position in relation to the Guermantes, as the Affair deepens his identification with his Jewish roots, is one of the great threads running through the novel. It is paralleled within the Guermantes family itself by the fate of another prominent member, the duke's brother, the Baron de Charlus. Charlus, who rejoices in the unusual name Palamède (one of a number of gloriously eccentric Christian names borne by Proust's aristos), is the second of the great protagonists of the novel – a creature of huge contradictions, ferocious temper, sudden unpredictable kindnesses, who veers wildly from the most extreme rudeness to the grandest of society ladies to acts of enormous generosity to servants, shopkeepers and their children. The narrator's first encounters with the Baron, who at one moment appears to offer him the most ardent friendship, only to withdraw it petulantly the next, leave him thoroughly bewildered. It is only when he catches sight of Charlus unawares, in a mysterious exchange of signals with the tailor who has a shop in the courtyard just below the narrator's apartment, that he realizes there is a psycho-sexual basis for the Baron's odd behaviour:

For what did I see! Face to face, in that courtyard where they had certainly not met before . . . the Baron, having suddenly opened wide his half-shut eyes, was gazing with extraordinary attentiveness at the ex-tailor poised on the threshold of his shop, while the latter, rooted suddenly to the spot in front of M. de Charlus, implanted there like a tree, contemplated with a look of wonderment the plump form of the ageing Baron . . . The Baron, who now sought to disguise the impression that had been made on him, and yet, in spite of his affectation of indifference, seemed unable to move away without regret, came and went, looked vaguely into the distance in the way which he felt would most enhance the beauty of his eyes, and assumed a smug, nonchalant, fatuous air. Meanwhile Jupien [the ex-tailor] . . . had – in perfect symmetry with the Baron – drawn back his head, set his torso at an advantageous angle, placed his fist on his hip with a grotesque impertinence and made his behind stick out, striking poses with the coquettishness that the orchid might have had for the providential advent of the bumblebee.

The orchid and the bumblebee are not fortuitous. Before this scene of homoerotic courtship, the narrator has been keenly anticipating the arrival of a bee to fertilize an orchid in the courtyard. He is struck by the parallels between plant fertilization and human sexual activity, including between the self-fertilization of certain flowers and homosexual encounters of the kind he has just observed. In fact, the first part of the fourth book, *Sodom and Gomorrah*, consists of an extended reflection, sparked off by this incident, on the phenomenon of homosexuality (a term the narrator finds as inadequate as the other contemporary term he uses for a homosexual: 'invert') in humans and analogous phenomena in the world of plants. Orchids were extraordinarily fashionable in Paris in the last decade of the nineteenth century and Proust uses the flower not only to provide a subtle and complex correspondence in the vegetable world to Charlus's act of sterile fertilization with Jupien, but also as the emblem that Swann and his mistress choose for their physical love-making.

From this point on, homosexual attraction and desire develop as major themes of the novel, one of their chief interests for the narrator being the way they act as a great leveller between the classes, exemplified by the Baron's later reckless infatuation with a young man whose grandfather had been a manservant of the narrator's great-uncle.

As for Gomorrah, and the devotees of Sapphic love, the (hetero-sexual) narrator is allowed – except for one brief scene very early in the book – no direct access to this world. He can catch only half-glimpses of it from hints and suggestions, rumour and hearsay, which, when the tales and hints relate to the objects of his obsessive desire, reduce him (and Swann before him) to a near-manic state of jealousy. The fifth of the seven books of *Remembrance of Things Past* is largely devoted to the narrator's tortured attempt to gain complete control of an impoverished orphan girl, Albertine, whom he main-tains and keeps captive in his Paris apartment. The attempt is doomed to failure, since other human beings are unknowable:

> I could, if I chose, take Albertine on my knee, hold her head in my hands, I could caress her, run my hands slowly over her, but, just as if I had been handling a stone which encloses the salt of immemorial oceans or the light of a star, I felt that I was touching no more than the sealed envelope of a person who inwardly reached to infinity.

By the end of the sixth book of *Remembrance of Things Past*, this 'I' for whom Albertine, and all others, are so unfathomable – our narrator – has learned that it is neither in society nor in love that he will find the key to the happiness he seeks. He must look elsewhere.

A final article on Proust's novel will follow in issue 58.

ANTHONY WELLS has spent the best part of a lifetime avoiding putting pen to paper, prevaricating with a number of occupations including monitoring East German radio for the BBC, librarianship and running a family business. He hopes it's going to be a case of better late than never.

Journey to the Interior

KEN HAIGH

The Japanese poet Matsuo Basho (1644–94) is renowned in the West as a master of haiku, but less well known is the fact that he was also a superb travel writer. He wrote five travel diaries, of which the last, *Oku no Hosomichi* (*The Narrow Road to the Deep North*, 1702), is considered his masterpiece.

There have been many English translations of this work. Indeed, the problem with recommending Basho to an English readership is in recommending a translation. I first encountered Basho's journal in Dorothy Britton's translation when I was a teenager. I stumbled upon it in my local public library, and it quickly became one of my favourite books, one I would borrow again and again. If I now find Britton's work a little stiff (Britton, for example, insisted on writing the haiku in rhyme, as she felt this helped 'to suggest the formal elegance achieved in the original'), that is perhaps more a reflection of how my tastes have changed over the years than any slight on the excellence of her translation. Donald Keene's translation is also very good, as is Sam Hammill's (he does a fine job translating the poetry), but perhaps the easiest to find is the translation by Nobuyuki Yuasa in the Penguin Classics series, so that is the one I will use here. This is how Yuasa translates the opening passage:

> Days and months are travellers of eternity. So are the years that pass by. Those who steer a boat across the sea, or drive a horse

Matsuo Basho, *The Narrow Road to the Deep North* (1702) · Trans. Nobuyuki Yuasa · Penguin · Pb · 176pp · £7.99 · ISBN 9780140441857 over the earth till they succumb to the weight of years, spend every minute of their lives travelling. There are a great number of ancients, too, who died on the road. I myself have been tempted for a long time by the cloud-moving wind – filled with a strong desire to wander.

It was only towards the end of last autumn that I returned from rambling along the coast. I barely had time to sweep the cobwebs from my broken house on the River Sumida before the New Year, but no sooner had the spring mist begun to rise over the field than I wanted to be on the road again to cross the barrier-gate of Shirakawa in due time. The gods seem to have possessed my soul and turned it inside out, and roadside images seemed to invite me from every corner, so that it was impossible for me to stay idle at home. Even while I was getting ready, mending my torn trousers, tying a new strap to my hat, and applying *moxa* to my legs to strengthen them, I was already dreaming of the full moon rising over the islands of Matsushima. Finally, I sold my house, moving to the cottage of Sampū for a temporary stay. Upon the threshold of my old home, however, I wrote a linked verse of eight pieces and hung it on a wooden pillar. The starting piece was:

> Behind this door
> Now buried in deep grass,
> A different generation will celebrate
> The Festival of Dolls.

Basho explains that he is motivated to make this difficult journey by his desire to see the places, like Matsushima, celebrated by earlier poets, much as we might aspire to visit the Lake District to see the landscape made famous by Wordsworth. But there is clearly more at stake here. This is not a holiday. To begin with, the journey Basho proposes will not be an easy one. The districts he wishes to visit were, in his day, considered remote and difficult to reach. Travelling by foot and occasionally on horseback, his journey will take him six months. He sells his house and its contents, shaves his head, dresses like an itinerant Buddhist priest, and carries all of his worldly possessions on his back. He does not intend to return. This journey has an air of finality to it, even desperation. At several points in the narrative, he despairs of surviving the journey, writing that if he were to die on his way to the far north, 'it would only be the fulfilment of providence'.

What is his motivation then? Part of the answer might lie in the title. *Hosomichi* means 'narrow road', but *Oku* has several meanings. In general, it refers to the northern part of Honshu, the largest of Japan's islands, but it can also mean 'interior' or 'interior region'. Perhaps Basho is telling us that he is making two journeys: an outer journey to this remote region of Japan and an inner journey of self-abnegation towards poetic clarity. Basho, a follower of Zen Buddhism, must try to see and describe the landscape as it truly is. There can be no laziness. He must not fall back on literary shortcuts or tricks. Everything must be seen with fresh eyes and described precisely. Only in this way will he discover the true nature of reality.

The form Basho follows is called *haibun*, a mixture of poetry and prose. To write *haibun* well, the two forms must work together. The poetry should not feel tacked on to the prose, for it is through the poetry that Basho can attempt to express the inexpressible. Take the poem quoted above, for example. The Festival of Dolls, also known as Girls' Day, is a day for Japanese families to pray for the welfare of their daughters. Mothers and daughters mark the occasion by decorating their houses with rows of dolls. These dolls are family heirlooms, passed from one generation of women to the next. On the surface, Basho is making a simple observation: the house has changed ownership. Basho, a bachelor, has sold his house to a man with daughters who will celebrate the Festival of Dolls. But looked at again we realize that this is a poem about transience. Basho is reminding us that nothing stays the same. We should not become too attached to things. Even the mention of grass in the yard reminds us that one day his thatched hut will decay and disappear.

Basho encounters hardships on his journey. At one point, storm-stayed in a mountain pass, he is forced to spend three days in the rude hut of a gatekeeper:

> Bitten by fleas and lice,
> I slept in a bed,
> A horse urinating all the time
> Close to my pillow.

At times, he is hungry, weary and half-frozen, and twice he complains about the flare-up of an 'old complaint', about which he remains vague.

But there are also moments of bright fellowship on the road, meetings with friends old and new, evenings of song and wine spent composing poetry. Basho records the kindnesses he is shown, like the farmer who takes pity on him and lends him his horse, telling him to turn the beast loose when he reaches the next village, for the animal will find its way home; or the painter Basho meets, who takes him in, shows him all the local sites – which Basho would otherwise have missed – and then, upon his departure, gives him a farewell gift of a hand-drawn map to guide him on his way and a new pair of sandals, with straps dyed blue, to match the irises for which the district is famed:

> It looks as if
> Iris flowers had bloomed
> On my feet –
> Sandals laced in blue.

There is also the innkeeper called Honest Gozaemon, whom Basho found 'almost stubbornly honest, utterly devoid of worldly cleverness. It was as if the merciful Buddha himself had taken the shape of man to help me in my wandering pilgrimage.'

To offset the hardships of the journey, there are moments of rare beauty. Basho loves the natural world. He is frequently moved by what he sees, and sometimes a poem is the best way to capture this sense of the sublime, as in this moment, watching the sun set at the mouth of the Mogami River:

> The River Mogami has drowned
> Far and deep
> Beneath its surging waves
> The flaming sun of summer.

These moments of wonder are balanced by moments of pathos. Many of the historic sites Basho seeks lie in ruins, covered in grass and decay: a reminder, should the reader need one, of the vanity of human wishes. At one temple, he is shown the helmet of a famous warrior, who was killed in battle fighting his former masters. 'The helmet was certainly an extraordinary one, with an arabesque of gold chrysanthemums covering the visor and the ear-plate, a fiery dragon resting proudly on the crest, and two curved horns pointing to the sky.' As he contemplates the beautiful object and reflects on the career of the man who wore it, Basho notes:

> I am awe-struck
> To hear a cricket singing
> Underneath the dark cavity
> Of an old helmet.

His account is clean and simple, the prose and poetry precise and crisp. The writing gives the appearance of effortlessness, as if it was just jotted down as he walked along. But it wasn't. We know this because Basho did not travel alone. For a good portion of his journey he was accompanied by a poetry student, his disciple Sora, who also kept a journal of their expedition. By comparing the journals, scholars have been able to see where Basho compresses incidents, and even changes the chronology slightly in order to give the composition balance. It will take Basho four years to complete this short narrative. Stricken with wanderlust, Basho never does settle down. In fact, his great masterpiece will be published posthumously; for having completed it, he sets out on the road once again, this time to visit Ueno, Kyoto and Osaka. Overcome on the way with a stomach ailment, possibly dysentery, he dies, homeless, but surrounded by his disciples. His final poem:

> Seized with a disease
> Halfway on the road,
> My dreams keep revolving
> Round the withered moor.

I will probably never travel to Japan – or learn Japanese for that matter – but something about this simple journal speaks to me across the span of three hundred years. In Basho, I sense a kindred spirit. I understand his restlessness and his love of the natural world. I admire the economy of his prose and the precision of his poetry. I love Basho because I can reread this short work over and over and never cease to find something new to admire.

KEN HAIGH is a librarian in southern Ontario, and, like Basho, he suffers from itchy feet. He dreams of some day taking a really long walk, the Appalachian Trail, the Camino de Santiago or perhaps a stroll from Canterbury to Jerusalem.

The Man Who Enjoyed Everything

DEREK PARKER

If Sir Edward Marsh appears in a few literary reference books, it is as the editor of five anthologies of Georgian poetry published between 1911 and 1922, the idea for which came from Rupert Brooke. As Brooke said, they 'went up like a rocket'; 'Yes, and came down like a stick,' Marsh ruefully recalled. But his name pops up unexpectedly – usually just as 'Eddie' – in many memoirs and biographies of twentieth-century figures from Henry James to Ivor Novello, Somerset Maugham to David Cecil, D. H. to T. E. Lawrence. And he was for a quarter of a century the close friend and assistant of Winston Churchill.

He had an enormous talent for friendship, a lesser talent for discretion, and a love of a good story – displayed almost relentlessly in his memoir *A Number of People*, which came out in 1939. I bought my copy at least fifty years ago, from the tray outside Sheila Ramage's wonderful bookshop just along the street in Notting Hill. It's still marked 1/6, in pencil, and was certainly second-hand, if not third- or fourth-. The cover fell off on the way home. Did I really want it? Always a sucker for a good anecdote, it didn't take me long to decide.

Born in 1872, the son of a surgeon who became Master of Downing College, Cambridge, Eddie was fortunate in his mother, who read to him incessantly – he heard all the Waverley novels and all the major novels of Dickens between the ages of 10 and 12. He had a brilliant

---

Edward Marsh, *A Number of People* (1939), is out of print but we can obtain second-hand copies.

career at Cambridge, during which he excelled in Latin and Greek, passing the time while waiting for the papers to be turned out on the morning of an examination by making an elegant Latin translation of Wordsworth's sonnet on Westminster Bridge.

He went into the Civil Service, and worked as a Private Secretary to a succession of Britain's most powerful ministers, beginning with Joseph Chamberlain. Much of his career was spent with Churchill, following him to every department he occupied until 1929. He got on as well with his master as they both did with Ivor Novello, and recalls an evening during which his two friends competed with each other in singing the music-hall songs of the 1880s – Ivor remembered all the tunes, while Churchill remembered all the lyrics.

Whether Eddie rivalled Ivor in looks is questionable – in charm, clearly, but though some friends called him handsome, both his portrait by his friend Neville Lytton and a bust by Frank Dobson seem to focus almost entirely on what Graham Sutherland described as 'those extraordinary upturned eyebrows' which another friend termed 'elfin'. Everyone agreed on his 'high, light, slightly lisping, withdrawn yet infinitely persuasive voice, the quizzical regard and the tensed elegant body' (Sutherland again), and Max Beerbohm drew him as an immaculately dressed figure with a monocle on a gold chain and four official keys dangling from another, silver one.

His persuasive tact no doubt helped him in his career as a highly efficient civil servant. His knighthood, conferred on him in private audience by King George at a second attempt – he forgot to go to Buckingham Palace on the first date given him – was for services to Government. His heart, however, was in books, art and the theatre – and in making friends, some rich, some poor. Staying with Neville Lytton in his Paris studio they spent a whole night dropping bedbugs into a bath of insecticide, 'in which they swam about triumphantly, like Rhine-Maidens, and in the end had to be burnt'. Maurice Baring however had enough money to indulge in such expensive jokes as producing an exquisite leather-bound book for his friends which,

Sir Edward Marsh by Howard Coster, 1939
© NPG

when opened, proved to consist only of a single page bearing the Lord's Prayer, with a loose ticket stating that it came 'With the author's compliments'.

No snob, Eddie certainly loved a lord – and a lady – and the more eccentric they were the more they delighted him. He either remembered their conversation vividly or jotted down the most memorable phrases in the small notebook he always carried. His friend Mrs Asquith (a.k.a. Margot Tennant, a.k.a. Lady Oxford) had a unique turn of phrase, 'calling a visitor who "put on" a relentless American accent "an imitation rough diamond"'. Of another acquaintance, 'so-and-so told enough white lies to ice a cake', and of a certain politician, 'of course he can't see a belt without hitting below it'. Asked whether she believed in ghosts, she answered, 'Appearances are in their favour.'

One of his closest friends was Lady Betty Balfour, whose general affability got her into trouble: she 'once rode on the top of an omnibus all the way from Piccadilly Circus to Addison Road in colloquy with a working-man whose wife had just died, leaving him with a number of small children. Such was the sympathy and wisdom with which she counselled him that just before she reached her stop he asked her to marry him.'

Eddie was an unobtrusive homosexual, but even during his lifetime there were certainly clues. *A Number of People* is illustrated with photographs which surely must have told a story, even in 1939 – there is little to choose, for stunning profiles, between Neville Lytton, Patrick Shaw-Stewart, Ivor Novello and Rupert Brooke. But he is of course reticent in what he wrote of them – and he barely mentions the painter Mark Gertler, with whom he had a passionate and turbulent relationship. Brooke, by general consent the most beautiful young man in England, was the love of his life, but sadly for him was not gay. However their friendship was deep, as their letters reveal, and Eddie's introductory essay to Brooke's poems, published posthumously, remains probably the most perceptive assessment of him.

The Russell brothers were also close friends. Claude and Gilbert had profiles like Greek statues. Claude, having difficulty in packing his clothes after a weekend, remarked, 'It's astonishing how much more room dirty clothes take than clean ones – quite out of proportion to the amount of dirt;' while Gilbert, discussing money with his friend the Aga Khan, recalled him saying, 'I suppose a thousand pounds to me is about the same as sixpence to you.' Gilbert promptly produced a half-crown and said, 'Would you mind giving me change for this?'

Eddie's taste in books was catholic: on a visit to Paris, he came back with a clandestine copy of *Lady Chatterley's Lover* but found himself 'quite unable to get through it', and lent it to T. E. Lawrence, who wrote: 'I'm re-reading it with a slow, deliberate carelessness, trying to fancy I've never read a D. H. L. before . . . [he] has always been so rich and ripe a writer to me, before, that I'm deeply puzzled and hurt by this Lady Chatterley of his. Surely the sex business isn't worth all this damned fuss? I've only met a handful of people who really cared a biscuit for it.' Eddie more or less rescued D. H. from the authorities during the war, when he was accused of being a

German spy. There is nothing about that in the book, and he was discreet enough not to say anything illuminating about life at the Foreign Office. His account of his 1908 travels with Churchill to British East Africa, Uganda, the Sudan and Egypt is, sadly, not especially vivid (though he was pleased when the elder of a Ugandan tribe called him Bwana Balozui, or 'Big Noise', because he looked 'much the fiercest' of the group of diplomats).

He published verse translations of La Fontaine and Horace, edited several of Churchill's books and was considered the best proofreader of his time. Among the authors who sent him their galleys and proofs were Maugham, David Cecil and Harold Nicolson. 'To the onlie begetter of the ensuing commas,' one of them inscribed a presentation copy; but, though he felt passionately about punctuation, he loved a good, readable style. 'You don't listen to what you are writing, you don't listen enough,' he would cry plaintively in his high, insistent voice. And his marginal comments were remorseless: 'You really must have been feeling very tired when you wrote this chapter,' or more tersely, 'What on earth is this supposed to mean?'

If *A Number of People* is enjoyable to read, Eddie's life was clearly enjoyable to live. He enjoyed his work, he enjoyed his friends, he enjoyed his life – everything about it. He enjoyed theatre 'like a child', and was completely undiscerning. When Arnold Bennett had a new play on, and the critic James Agate told him, 'Eddie Marsh enjoyed it,' Bennett replied, 'Hang Eddie Marsh. He's a miserable fellow – he enjoys everything.'

'I should rather like that on my tombstone,' wrote Eddie.

DEREK PARKER now lives in Sydney, walking the dogs, enjoying not having to chip ice off the car windscreen, and waiting eagerly for the next issue of *Slightly Foxed* to suggest new reading matter.

A Boy in a Tattered Coat

ANN WROE

The little book didn't belong to me. I was made aware of this every day by the tight crimson boards, the gold letters clumsily punched on the spine, and above all by the label glued inside, which proclaimed it the property of Kingston-upon-Thames Public Libraries, Surbiton Branch. The two stags rampant that held the borough arms had a sly but threatening, possibly telltale, look. A long succession of dates of around 1961–2 was stamped on the facing label. They were all my renewals, for I had taken possession of this book, and couldn't let it go until it had surrendered all the magic I knew it contained.

The name of the author, Henry Williamson, had drawn my 11-year-old eyes to it at first. I already knew his work, for my parents' two-shelf library – containing *The English Counties*, *Gardening and Home Production*, their pharmaceutical textbooks and *Three Men in a Boat* – also had India-paper wartime editions of three of his 'Flax of Dream' novels, *The Beautiful Years*, *Dandelion Days* and *The Pathway*. I had not bothered with the last, because I sensed it was about love and grown-ups; then, as now, I would always rather see the world through the eyes of a child. The other volumes, achingly light and thin in their green covers, I adored with a passion. Willie Maddison, the young hero, was exactly me, suffering through imprisonment in school while longing to roam the North Devon woods and fields. The intensity of the writing, with its loving details of birds, flowers, scenes and weather, was all the more thrilling because

Henry Williamson, *The Star-Born* (1933), is out of print but we can obtain second-hand copies.

I was beginning to understand that I could try to do this myself. Every page added to my store of shining, tactile images and words.

I was very far from North Devon in Surbiton, with its streets of 1930s semis and numbing suburban ways, but I was an inveterate tomboy, my spare time spent much as Willie's was: wandering alone for hours over the Green Belt, blackberrying, fishing for minnows, climbing trees and trying to ride any bicycle I found abandoned, since I was barred from having one of my own. The heavy inevitability of being a girl was something I tried to forget. I emerged once from *Dandelion Days*, which I'd been reading surreptitiously in an upstairs classroom thick with the smell of polished linoleum, to find Susan Pinsent and Paula Ogden excitedly discussing bras and breasts. I was desperate never to have either, and clung to Willie Maddison as my alter ego until, a few years later, I became defiant, dangerous Stephen Daedalus, in my mind at least.

The little crimson-swaddled book I had discovered was not obviously part of the series I knew. It seemed to be a curious offshoot of the same time and place, in the same language and landscape but not in the same mood: a book of puzzlement and disquiet. I learned from the introduction that Williamson did consider it a 'pendant' (then a puzzling word) to the other books, and had put it together from memories of a lost manuscript read aloud one evening in his cottage in Devon. Faber first published it (I learned long afterwards) in 1933, and then again, in a revised version with new illustrations by Mildred Eldridge, in 1948. The 1948 edition was the one I had – or, rather, the one the library used to have.

That first reading by Williamson to his friends, gathered close round an open fire, the wind no doubt keening across the moors beyond the walls, would have suited the story well, for the whole book was suffused with night. The sketchy line drawings, which I examined first, were mostly of blasted moorland, wind-riven trees and the skulls of birds. Excitement lay there, but not without a touch of dread.

The book was called *The Star-Born*. Its first chapters were about owls, especially one called Eldrich, which sounded to me like the shriek of doom heard before a death. The owls were frightening: hunting, nipping on the neck, tearing open and gobbling down a succession of soft small rodents whose long tails dangled from their beaks, and whose tiny bones made an ossuary of the ruins where they nested. The next chapters were filled with creatures who were nebulous and filmy: Leaf Spirit, Air Spirit, Water Spirit and Quill Spirit, who lived among the dripping ferns and sunbows of the gorge of the River Lyd. Unable to visualize them, I could only hear their high pattering voices, addressing each other with churchy Thees and Thous to debate creation, life, past ages and their own importance.

Not caring much for the owls or the spirits, I skipped a fair amount at this stage. But I kept going, because what had seized and held me as I first looked through was a full-page picture of a ragged figure, a thin young man with dishevelled hair and dark eyes, who held a dead robin in his hand and was swirled about with mist, or light. This was the Star-born. His mother, the spirits had mentioned, was the Morning Star; he had been sent as a human baby, but had been snatched away to be brought up by owls. Now he had been sent again to instruct the earth in the way it should live. The picture already suggested, somehow, that he was going to fail.

No other image from my childhood so affected me. I looked at it again and again: the tattered coat, the bare feet, the beseeching eyes and the overpowering sense of sadness. He had fallen naked from the stars in a storm (narrowly missing a passing car), and had stolen his clothes from a scarecrow. He was clearly asking about the robin, but could speak no words beyond those others spoke to him, cleverly re-ordered and returned. At this point I was savouring every word about him, and especially the clash between this extraordinary figure and the ordinary country folk of North Devon. They, of course, could not make him out; he was mazed, an idiot, even a danger. In short order he liberated children from their classrooms, let goldfinches out of cages, saved hares from the huntsmen and tried to eat bread and butter with a knife and fork. (I was always being rebuked for my table manners; his were much, much worse!) Out in the wilds he was an uncontrolled child, heaving rocks into streams with cries of joy, and riding wildly on bicycles (again, like me) until he was unseated. He was, I suppose, the first in a long line of disruptive outsider-heroes: Daedalus, Hamlet, Raskolnikov, Mishkin, Mersault. Yet he was odder than any of those. When I read the book again, four decades later, he still seemed every bit as magical and bizarre.

For I did read it again, curious to revisit the spell it had cast over me. Having searched high and low for it in bookshops, I found it on Abebooks in two minutes, in its original jacket and, to preserve the mystery, an old tissue cover that misted the lettering. I took it on holiday to Glynde in East Sussex, the only book I packed for a week – which was peculiar, because I was in that febrile, anxious dip between writing projects when normally I read voraciously, cramming for the next idea. I must have had a feeling that it would be enough for me: a sense that it would unlock so many thoughts and associations, long buried away, that I would need nothing else.

Mildred Eldridge

One day I sat with it out in the courtyard, under the apple trees in the sun. After much the same half-creepy, half-perplexing journey, I was enjoying it now that 'the Boy', as everyone called him, had shown up. I was almost at the end, having forgotten the end, at the point where the Boy's earth-sister, Mamis, pulls a volume of poetry from the shelf and opens it. The lines she sees are from Shelley's 'Ode to the West Wind':

> If I were a dead leaf thou mightest bear;
> If I were a swift cloud to fly with thee;
> A wave to pant beneath thy power, and share
> The impulse of thy strength, only less free
> Than thou, O uncontrollable! . . .
> A heavy weight of hours has chain'd and bow'd
> One too like thee: tameless, and swift, and proud.

The parallel was meant to be with the Star-born, but for me it was as if I had never read the lines before. They struck me with such force that I seemed to be picked up and hurled through the air myself, and I immediately realized that I had to write the life of this poet – a poet who could live and move with spirits of water, leaves and air. Within the hour I had driven to Brighton to buy Shelley's collected verse; within two years I had produced *Being Shelley*.

I've often told the story of this wild moment, without ever mentioning which book I was reading at the time. My childhood treasure became a filter for inspiration in a way I could never have imagined. And when I turned back later to the picture I had so loved, the one of the Star-born standing in his tattered coat, I realized at once that the face I was looking at, near enough, was Shelley's.

ANN WROE is the Obituaries writer of *The Economist* and the author of seven books, including *Pilate*, *Being Shelley* and, most recently, *Six Facets of Light*.

GBS and Me

MICHAEL LEAPMAN

My enthusiasm for George Bernard Shaw dates from 1950, when I was 12. On my way home from school it was my habit to buy a copy of the *Star*, one of London's three evening papers, principally to check the cricket scores. One afternoon the front-page splash carried the bold headline: BERNARD SHAW DEAD. At the age of 94 he had fallen off a ladder while pruning his cherry tree, and he did not recover.

I reasoned that a man who warranted front-page treatment must be a writer of consequence, so I resolved to discover more. In a second-hand bookshop I found a copy of *Everybody's Political What's What*, written in 1944, and began to read.

I found it riveting. The first chapter is entitled 'Is human nature incurably depraved?' and begins: 'If it is, reading this book will be a waste of time, and it should be exchanged at once for a detective story or some pleasant classic, depending on your taste.' How better to grab the attention of a boy just starting to realize that politics is fairly important, and that trying to get to grips with it could be entertaining as well as instructive? The book's style, though mischievous, is trenchant and persuasive. Shaw was nearly 90 when he wrote it, yet he had retained the clarity that, as I would discover, imbues his books, his plays and their long, argumentative prefaces.

Everybody's Political What's What covers all conceivable (and some barely conceivable) aspects of public policy. Shaw was a Fabian socialist of a distinctive genre. He supported equality and democracy but was sharply critical of the political party system and of most professions, including medicine, banking, religion, economics and any activity connected to warfare. I quickly decided that his political views would be mine as well. He had addressed many of those themes in his plays, which I began to buy in the maroon and white uniform Penguin Plays editions – still in print, although now in a different livery. Later I started to collect Constable's 'standard edition' of the works, introduced in 1931, with their neat red and green lettering on cream jackets, protecting a rust-coloured binding.

The first of his plays I saw performed was *Androcles and the Lion*, in a school production. I wasn't in it, although I coveted the role of the Lion, who had only to roar and to hold up a paw for the pesky thorn to be removed before embracing Androcles in a friendly clinch. The preface makes clear that the play is essentially a sideways look at Christianity, but I doubt that I then appreciated the nuances.

In preparing to write this piece I consulted some of the volumes in the dedicated Shaw bookcase in our guest room. (Sadly, I can't detect that our guests make much use of it.) Inside the Penguin edition of *The Doctor's Dilemma* I discovered the programme of a production at the Theatre Royal, Brighton, that I had seen with my parents in September 1956. It was on its pre-West End tour and the cast included some of the theatrical greats of the time: Sir Lewis Casson (then over 80), Laurence Hardy, Michael Hordern, Ann Todd and Paul Daneman. Seat prices ranged from two shillings (10p) to 12s 6d. (62.5p).

The programme reveals that this was part of a Shaw autumn binge at the Theatre Royal, with two more productions of his plays scheduled for October: the one-acters *Fanny's First Play* and *Village Wooing* in a double bill starring Brenda Bruce, followed by *The Devil's Disciple*, played by Tyrone Power. Over my lifetime Shaw has come in and out of fashion among the literati, and the Fifties must have been a period when his work was thought highly relevant. Frustratingly I was unable to catch the other two productions, since October was the month of my call-up for two years' National Service in the Royal Navy.

During the second half of my service I was stationed at Chatham, convenient for jaunts to London. By then I had become a regular reader of the *New Statesman* (I still am) and noticed in it an advertisement for the Shaw Society, which discussed the works of the master at monthly meetings in a room in Albemarle Street, Mayfair. I joined eagerly, and once or twice amused the other disciples by turning up in my uniform, bell-bottomed trousers and all. After the meetings we would adjourn for a cup of tea, a cigarette and more earnest Shavian talk at Lyons Corner House on Piccadilly Circus.

In 1958 the musical *My Fair Lady*, based on Shaw's *Pygmalion*, opened at the Theatre Royal, Drury Lane, and the society made a block booking. From the theatre's upper reaches we watched Rex Harrison, Julie Andrews and Stanley Holloway going through their paces. Although we were predisposed to disapprove of any undue tampering with the hallowed text, we had to agree that the show was a success, primarily because so much of Shaw's dialogue had in fact survived.

Even some of Alan Jay Lerner's spirited lyrics are rooted in the play's script. Shaw's Higgins declares: 'Women upset everything. When you let them into your life you find that the woman is driving at one thing and you're driving at another.' Lerner translates this as

> Let a woman in your life
> And you are up against the wall!
> Make a plan and you will find
> She has something else in mind . . .

Again, Lerner's Higgins laments in song:

> An Englishman's way of speaking absolutely
> classifies him.
> The moment he talks he makes some other
> Englishman despise him.

– an almost direct quotation from Shaw's preface.

I have of course seen many productions of *My Fair Lady* since then, most notably an Icelandic version in Reykjavik in the early Sixties. Translating 'The rain in Spain stays mainly in the plain' into Icelandic must have been a challenge, but to judge from the audience reaction it was met triumphantly.

My wife Olga does not wholly share my devotion to Shaw ('Too wordy') but she has generously indulged it for more than half a century, and we have together seen a large part of the canon. Sometimes our quest has taken us to unlikely places: I remember watching a fine performance of *The Dark Lady of the Sonnets* in a tiny room over a south London pub, with the rain dripping through a corner of the ceiling. During the Seventies we lived for some years in New York, where Shaw's sharp intellect was in tune with the city's *Zeitgeist* and his plays turned up regularly off Broadway.

Every summer an outdoor production of one of the works is staged on the lawn of Shaw's Corner in Ayot St Lawrence, Hertfordshire, where he lived from 1906 until his death. We have twice taken picnics there. On the first visit we saw *Too True to Be Good*, one of his weirder plays. It begins with a plaintive speech from 'The Monster', a character described in the author's stage directions as resembling a human being 'but in substance it seems of luminous jelly'. He turns out to be a microbe, complaining of having caught measles from an ailing young woman. Also involved is a man named Meek, who arrives on a motorbike in a colonial outpost and is based loosely on T. E. Lawrence, or Lawrence of Arabia.

Like many Shaw plays it goes on a bit. By the time it ended, with a three-page speech from the main character, the sun had set, the wine had run out and we were pulling the rug around ourselves ever tighter. Undaunted, we went back a couple of years later to see *The Apple Cart*. This is about a feud between a king and his prime minister, bearing some similarity to the recent West End hit *Charles III*. Thankfully, the night was balmier and the play shorter than on that first visit.

Over the years the National Theatre has produced its share of Shaw's plays. The late Peter Hall, its director from 1973 to 1988, was fond of them, so there was no lack of revivals during his tenure. I remember in particular the 1975 production of *Heartbreak House*, my favourite of them all, reflecting the upheavals in British society in the wake of the First World War. Colin Blakely gave a wonderful performance as the dissolute Captain Shotover, albeit not as moving as Richard Griffiths in the role at the Almeida in Islington in 1997. After leaving the National, Hall for some years directed an annual short season at the Theatre Royal, Bath, where a Shaw play was invariably part of the repertoire. Olga and I enjoyed our day trips to Somerset to catch them.

In 2002 Hall gave his daughter Rebecca her West End break in a splendid production of *Mrs Warren's Profession*, an early work, written in 1893. She played Mrs Warren's daughter Vivie – one of the many spirited, opinionated young heroines Shaw created in an era when feminism was in its infancy.

Nicholas Hytner, who took over at the National in 2003, admits in his recent memoir, *Balancing Acts*, that he had reservations about Shaw: 'I recognized his importance, even if I dreaded having to sit through endless performances.' His conversion came through *Saint Joan*, which he staged in 2007: 'From *Saint Joan* we had learned how little credence to give the old charge that Shaw was without passion. His people throb with the visceral excitement of argument. If an actor commits to it body and soul, argument becomes as passionate as a declaration of love.'

Saint Joan was quickly followed at the National by *Major Barbara* in 2008, but then came a hiatus. I happened to meet Hytner at a party in 2011 and suggested to him that it was time to revisit the works of the bearded sage. He asked what play he should mount and I replied that I hadn't seen *Candida* for a while. He chose *The Doctor's Dilemma*, then *Man and Superman*.

The enterprising Orange Tree Theatre in Richmond has been fertile ground for GBS groupies, often at times of comparative drought elsewhere. The plays, with their emphasis on impassioned dialogue rather than spectacle, adapt well to its square auditorium with seating on all four sides. In December it staged *Misalliance*, one of his more preposterous confections, written in 1910 and featuring an assertive Polish acrobat and pioneering aviatrix whose plane crashes into the greenhouse of a country house in Surrey, as well as an intended assassin who hides in a portable Turkish bath. The contemporary relevance of the play's powerful feminist message was duly underlined in a programme note. Nonetheless there were some in the audience, perhaps encountering Shaw for the first time, who manifestly found it all rather hard to take. They clearly identified with the final two lines, where the author slips in a characteristic joke against himself and his reputation for verbosity:

'I suppose there's nothing more to be said.'
'Thank goodness!'

MICHAEL LEAPMAN has been writing for national newspapers and magazines for sixty years, and is the author of seventeen books (all non-fiction).

Coming attractions

MARGARET DRABBLE sees Ireland through Trollope's eyes · NIGEL ANDREW discovers what happened to Elizabeth Jenkins · MAGGIE FERGUSSON meets Colin Thubron · MICHAEL HOLROYD enjoys the biography of an extraordinary biographer · VICTORIA NEUMARK finds consolation in Elizabeth Goudge · CHRISTOPHER RUSH witnesses a cosmic event · SUE GEE is drawn by E. H. Shepard · ROBIN BLAKE loses himself in the sixteenth century

Bibliography

The *Slightly Foxed* Crossword No. 9: Answers

Across: 1 SAXE-COBURG   6 VLAD   10 EUROA   11 ELEPHANTS   12 STEALTH   13 EARACHE   14 SYLVIA ROBSON   18 GILLIAN WYATT   21 PIZARRO   23 SILENCE   24 INANITION   25 CREDO   26 NUDE   27 BROADSWORD

Down 1 SMERSH   2 XERXES   3 CHARLEY KINRAID   4 BEETHOVEN   5 REEVE   7 LONGCASE   8 DISCERNS   9 CHARLOTTE LUCAS   15 ABYSSINIA   16 EGYPTIAN   17 BLIZZARD   19 ANGELO   20 DECOUD   22 OSIER